בְּכָל-לְבָבְךָ

With All Your Heart:
A *Shabbat* and Festival Companion

Edited and Translated by Rabbi Julie K. Gordon

MINNEAPOLIS JEWISH DAY SCHOOL

With All Your Heart:
A Shabbat and Festival Companion

is dedicated by

Jim & Nannette Greenfield and
Lynn Lederman & Ken Raskin

In honor of their children
David & Benjamin Greenfield
Sara and Ari Lederman
Daniel & Aaron Raskin

עַל שְׁלשָׁה דְבָרִים הָעוֹלָם עוֹמֵד:
עַל הַתּוֹרה וְעַל הָעֲבוֹדָה
וְעַל גְּמִילוּת חֲסָדִים.

"The world stands on three things:
the study of *Torah*, prayer to God,
and acts of loving kindness."

Mishnah Avot 1:2

FOREWORD

Aḥad HaAm, an advocate of cultural Zionism wrote, "More than the Jewish people have kept *Shabbat, Shabbat* has kept the Jewish people."

As Day School educators we want our next generation of children to continue to be kept by *Shabbat*. If we are to achieve this goal, we must be assured that the children acquire the knowledge of *Shabbat* rituals, *brakhot* (blessings), and *t'fillot* (prayers). We also believe that it is critical for children to understand these traditions and to find ways to explore the meanings of prayers.

We see parents as partners with school and synagogue in sharing the traditions of *Shabbat*. With All Your Heart: A *Shabbat* and Festival Companion was created to encourage families to enjoy meaningful *Shabbat* and Festival celebrations. These holy moments provide us with the opportunity to step back from the intensity of our moment-to-moment experiences and gain perspective on what is truly important. The rhythm of the Jewish week and calendar year aids us in expanding our appreciation for what is truly important and joyous in our lives.

This publication is an educational tool to encourage joyous and meaningful celebrations at school, home, and synagogue. At MJDS we are deeply committed to providing meaningful *Shabbat* and Festival celebrations that open the world of Jewish ritual and help our students and their parents create personal connections to our tradition.

בְּכָל־לְבָבְךָ With All Your Heart: A *Shabbat* and Festival Companion—is our attempt to provide learners of all ages with a guide that can enhance these connections:

- Engaging introductions and discussion suggestions focus on the meaning and structure of *Shabbat* and Festival rituals, providing entry pathways to participants of all ages.

- The layout of the Hebrew text is designed to capture the rhythms, music, and flow of the poetry of the prayers, helping the user to read with fluency. The large font and clear, bold text support emerging readers of Hebrew.

- English translations are accessible to children and adults alike and encourage understanding and discussions of *Shabbat* and Festival home liturgy. All language referring to God is gender neutral. Transliterations are included to welcome non-Hebrew readers and encourage them to participate in all rituals and *mitzvot* on their path to increasing spiritual involvement.

- Illustrations, all created by MJDS students, provide images reflecting the conceptual meanings of prayers and rituals. They underscore aesthetic and non-verbal ways of engaging with *Shabbat* and Festival observances. It is our hope that these beautiful drawings will open the imaginations of participants, making our traditions more accessible for learners with both emerging and strong reading skills.

- "Open space" on many pages offers a place for each participant's individual images that may develop during *Shabbat* and Festival rituals and prayers that supplement one's approach to the written text.

- The Companion is designed to promote understanding of the structure of *Shabbat* and Festival rituals. Each *Shabbat* and Festival section is color-coded to offer visual cues. Highlighted colors in the text underscore unique features of prayers and help participants identify moments when the leader recites and the family or community responds. Additionally, sources for prayers and songs have been included to aid the reader's understanding of our traditions.

The preparation of With All Your Heart: A *Shabbat* and Festival Companion has been actively supported by the faculty and parents at the Minneapolis Jewish Day School. Community clergy aided us with their wisdom, insight, and talents. Our community is committed to creatively approaching the study and practice of *Shabbat* and Festivals, both at school and in the home and this is having a positive impact on the experiences of our students. Building a bridge between school, home, and synagogue is essential in creating and engaging the next generation of educated, committed, and observant Jews.

In particular, we want to express our gratitude to three MJDS faculty who went above and beyond in sharing their talents and skills in the preparation of With All Your Heart: A *Shabbat* and Festival Companion. We are appreciative of Sara Bernstein, Robert Portnoe, and Victoria Thor whose thoughtful suggestions, hours of creative activity, and editing helped shape the Companion.

This volume reflects the passionate commitment of Rabbi Julie Gordon to making *Shabbat* and Festival observance spiritually engaging and accessible. Her vision and attention to every detail reflect a desire to offer learners of all ages a guide that they can treasure.

Scholars observe that in biblical times, the heart was viewed as the place where the intellect resided. Now, the heart is seen as the seat of our emotional and spiritual capabilities. May this Companion help to facilitate meaningful *Shabbat* and Festival celebrations at school, in our homes, and in our synagogues. May it help us to grow intellectually and spiritually, bringing us closer to God, uplifting the spirits of learners, and enhancing our sense of Jewish community.

Ray Levi, Ph.D.
Head of School
MJDS

Rabbi Julie K. Gordon
Spiritual Life Director
MJDS

Tz'dakah

Generosity and Right Actions

צְדָקָה

It is traditional to give *tz'dakah* before the beginning of *Shabbat* and Festivals. We put money, a reminder of our work week, into a special *tz'dakah* box, sometimes called a *pushke*. This *mitzvah* teaches us to act justly by giving to those in need. As we give *tz'dakah*, we are sharing the responsibility for *tikkun olam* (improving our world). As you deposit the money and transition to your celebrations, offer a wish for the world, sing a song, or hum a *nigun* (melody without words).

· How do we transform donating *tz'dakah* into more than a routine asking for coins from a parent's pocket?

· How do we inspire giving *tz'dakah* to become a treasured part of our child's life?

· How do we teach them, when they receive their allowance, to allocate for *tz'dakah*, saving, and spending?

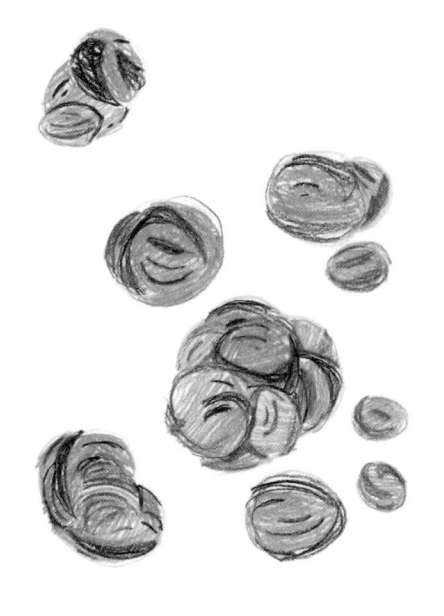

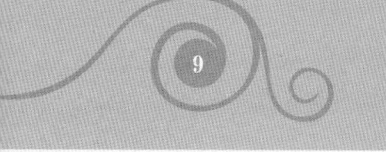

- Discuss with your children Jewish and non-Jewish organizations that have touched those you love and that you feel passionate about their work. Research how they will benefit from your *tz'dakah*.

- Once the *tz'dakah* box is full, if possible, deliver your gift in person. If visiting the organization isn't feasible, have your children sit with you as you write the checks and include your children's handwritten notes and pictures. Invite them to address the envelopes that contain your family's contributions.

- Helping others isn't only achieved by donating money. It is also fulfilled by donating your time or useful items–clothes, books, birthday gifts, and toys. There are many ways families with children of all ages can volunteer together to develop a life-long commitment to *tikkun olam* through community service.

הַדְלָקַת נֵרוֹת לְשַׁבָּת

Hadlakat Neirot L'Shabbat

Lighting *Shabbat* Candles

The *Shabbat* candles are symbols of hope and peace. As we light them, we mark the transition from the work week. The *brakhah* (blessing) we say over the candles expresses our thanks to God for the gift of *Shabbat*.

Traditionally, two candles are lit eighteen minutes before sunset. Some families light an extra candle for each member of the household. You can offer candles to your guests to enhance their *Shabbat* experience. It is a custom to bring the light of the candles into our hearts by circling our arms toward our face, one to seven times, and covering our eyes before reciting the *brakhah*.

בָּרוּךְ אַתָּה יְיָ אֱלֹהֵינוּ מֶלֶךְ הָעוֹלָם,
אֲשֶׁר קִדְּשָׁנוּ בְּמִצְוֹתָיו וְצִוָּנוּ,
לְהַדְלִיק נֵר שֶׁל שַׁבָּת.

Barukh atah Adonai Eloheinu melekh ha'olam, asher kid'shanu b'mitzvotav v'tzivanu, l'hadlik neir shel Shabbat.

Praised are You, *Adonai*, our God, Ruler of the universe,
You make us holy through Your *mitzvot* and command us to kindle the *Shabbat* lights.

Upon opening our eyes, the glowing *Shabbat* candles show us that we have physically and spiritually created *Shabbat*. After the *brakhah*, recite a personal prayer for family and friends. Offer a kiss, hug, or handshake, and joyfully wish each other *"Shabbat Shalom."*

· How can you increase a sense of peace in your family?

Shalom Aleikhem
Peace Unto You

שָׁלוֹם עֲלֵיכֶם

This traditional song contains images of two *mal'akhei hasharet* (angels) who visit to bless our home on *Shabbat*. They inspire us to become messengers of peace and to share our *Shabbat* joy with family and friends. Put your arms around each other, sway, and sing. "May peace come to you!"

שָׁלוֹם עֲלֵיכֶם,
מַלְאֲכֵי הַשָּׁרֵת
מַלְאֲכֵי עֶלְיוֹן,
מִמֶּלֶךְ מַלְכֵי הַמְּלָכִים
הַקָּדוֹשׁ בָּרוּךְ הוּא:

בּוֹאֲכֶם לְשָׁלוֹם,
מַלְאֲכֵי הַשָּׁלוֹם
מַלְאֲכֵי עֶלְיוֹן,
מִמֶּלֶךְ מַלְכֵי הַמְּלָכִים
הַקָּדוֹשׁ בָּרוּךְ הוּא:

בָּרְכוּנִי לְשָׁלוֹם, מַלְאֲכֵי הַשָּׁלוֹם
מַלְאֲכֵי עֶלְיוֹן, מִמֶּלֶךְ מַלְכֵי הַמְּלָכִים
הַקָּדוֹשׁ בָּרוּךְ הוּא:

צֵאתְכֶם לְשָׁלוֹם, מַלְאֲכֵי הַשָּׁלוֹם
מַלְאֲכֵי עֶלְיוֹן, מִמֶּלֶךְ מַלְכֵי הַמְּלָכִים
הַקָּדוֹשׁ בָּרוּךְ הוּא:

Shalom aleikhem, mal'akhei hasharet,
Mal'akhei Elyon, miMelekh Malkhei Ham'lakhim
HaKadosh Barukh Hu.

Bo'akhem l'shalom, mal'akhei hashalom
Mal'akhei Elyon, miMelekh Malkhei Ham'lakhim
HaKadosh Barukh Hu.

Barkhuni l'shalom mal'akhei hashalom
Mal'akhei Elyon, miMelekh Malkhei Ham'lakhim
HaKadosh Barukh Hu.

Tzeitkhem l'shalom, mal'akhei hashalom
Mal'akhei Elyon, miMelekh Malkhei Ham'lakhim
HaKadosh Barukh Hu.

Peace be to you angels, angels of the Most High,
From the Ruler, the Ruler of rulers, The Holy and Praised.

Come in peace, angels of peace,
Angels of the Most High,
From the Ruler, the Ruler of rulers,
The Holy and Praised.

Bless me with peace, angels of peace,
Angels of the Most High,
From the Ruler, the Ruler of rulers,
The Holy and Praised.

Go in peace, angels of peace, angels
Of the Most High, from the Ruler, the
Ruler of rulers, The Holy and Praised.

· What message does the angel have for you?

· What blessings do you want to ask the angel to bring to your
  home and to your guests?

· How do we welcome each other after a quarrel?

בִּרְכוֹת הַמִּשְׁפָּחָה
Birkhot Hamishpahah

Family Blessings

Through this custom parents express love for children. Place your hands on your child's head and offer this *brakhah* that originated when our ancestor Jacob blessed his grandsons, Ephraim and *M'nasheh*. We encourage our sons to be like them and our daughters to be inspired by our matriarchs Sarah, Rebekah, Rachel, and Leah.

To a son:

יְשִׂימְךָ אֱלֹהִים כְּאֶפְרַיִם וְכִמְנַשֶּׁה:

Y'simkha Elohim k'Efrayim v'khiM'nasheh.   Genesis 48:20

May God make you like Ephraim and M'nasheh.

To a daughter:

יְשִׂימֵךְ אֱלֹהִים כְּשָׂרָה רִבְקָה רָחֵל וְלֵאָה:

Y'simekh Elohim k'Sarah Rivkah Rahel v'Le'ah.

May God make you like Sarah, Rebekah, Rachel, and Leah.

Continue reciting the priestly benediction:

יְבָרֶכְךָ יְיָ וְיִשְׁמְרֶךָ:
יָאֵר יְיָ פָּנָיו אֵלֶיךָ וִיחֻנֶּךָּ:
יִשָּׂא יְיָ פָּנָיו אֵלֶיךָ וְיָשֵׂם לְךָ שָׁלוֹם:

Y'varekh'kha Adonai v'yishm'rekhah
Ya'er Adonai panav eileikhah vihunekkah
Yisa Adonai panav eleikhah v'yasem l'kha shalom.

May *Adonai* bless you and watch over you.
May *Adonai* give you light and compassion.
May *Adonai* accept your prayer and give you peace.

• Give a kiss, a hug, and add personal words of gratitude and insight into each child's uniqueness.

Blessing for Family and Friends

Some people hold hands as they recite the following *brakhah* asking God to grant peace for their family and friends:

הָרַחֲמָן הוּא יְבָרֵךְ אוֹתָנוּ כֻּלָּנוּ יַחַד בְּבִרְכַּת שָׁלוֹם.

Haraḥaman hu y'varekh otanu kulanu yaḥad b'virkat shalom.

May the Merciful One bless all of us with the blessing of peace.

Invite the children to honor the adults.

· How were you helped by this special adult this week?

אֵשֶׁת חַיִל

Eishet Ḥayil

A Woman of Valor

This passage from Proverbs sings the praises of a valiant woman. Jewish mystics interpreted this admiration to be directed toward the *Shabbat* Queen. A tradition developed for these verses to be sung by a husband to his wife at the *Shabbat* table. In modern times, both *Eishet Ḥayil* and *Ashrei Ha'ish* are opportunities to express love and respect from one partner to another. Some families chant the first few lines and continue humming the melody as a *nigun*.

אֵשֶׁת חַיִל מִי יִמְצָא,
וְרָחֹק מִפְּנִינִים מִכְרָהּ.
בָּטַח בָּהּ לֵב בַּעְלָהּ,
וְשָׁלָל לֹא יֶחְסָר.

Eishet ḥayil mi yimtzah, v'raḥok mip'ninim mikhrah. Bataḥ bah lev ba'lah, v'shalal lo yeḥsar.

A woman of valor is a rare find! She is more precious to him than rubies. Her husband trusts her, and lacks no good thing.

גְּמָלַתְהוּ טוֹב וְלֹא רָע, כֹּל יְמֵי חַיֶּיהָ.

דָּרְשָׁה צֶמֶר וּפִשְׁתִּים, וַתַּעַשׂ בְּחֵפֶץ כַּפֶּיהָ.

הָיְתָה כָּאֳנִיּוֹת סוֹחֵר, מִמֶּרְחָק תָּבִיא לַחְמָהּ.

וַתָּקָם בְּעוֹד לַיְלָה,

וַתִּתֵּן טֶרֶף לְבֵיתָהּ וְחֹק לְנַעֲרֹתֶיהָ.

זָמְמָה שָׂדֶה וַתִּקָּחֵהוּ, מִפְּרִי כַפֶּיהָ נָטְעָה כָּרֶם.

חָגְרָה בְעֹז מָתְנֶיהָ, וַתְּאַמֵּץ זְרוֹעֹתֶיהָ.

טָעֲמָה כִּי טוֹב סַחְרָהּ, לֹא יִכְבֶּה בַלַּיְלָה נֵרָהּ.

יָדֶיהָ שִׁלְּחָה בַכִּישׁוֹר, וְכַפֶּיהָ תָּמְכוּ פָלֶךְ.

כַּפָּהּ פָּרְשָׂה לֶעָנִי, וְיָדֶיהָ שִׁלְּחָה לָאֶבְיוֹן.

לֹא תִירָא לְבֵיתָהּ מִשָּׁלֶג, כִּי כָל בֵּיתָהּ לָבֻשׁ שָׁנִים.

מַרְבַדִּים עָשְׂתָה לָּהּ, שֵׁשׁ וְאַרְגָּמָן לְבוּשָׁהּ.

נוֹדָע בַּשְּׁעָרִים בַּעְלָהּ, בְּשִׁבְתּוֹ עִם זִקְנֵי אָרֶץ.

סָדִין עָשְׂתָה וַתִּמְכֹּר, וַחֲגוֹר נָתְנָה לַכְּנַעֲנִי.

עֹז וְהָדָר לְבוּשָׁהּ, וַתִּשְׂחַק לְיוֹם אַחֲרוֹן.

פִּיהָ פָּתְחָה בְחָכְמָה, וְתוֹרַת חֶסֶד עַל לְשׁוֹנָהּ.

צוֹפִיָּה הֲלִיכוֹת בֵּיתָהּ, וְלֶחֶם עַצְלוּת לֹא תֹאכֵל.

קָמוּ בָנֶיהָ וַיְאַשְּׁרוּהָ, בַּעְלָהּ וַיְהַלְלָהּ.

רַבּוֹת בָּנוֹת עָשׂוּ חָיִל, וְאַתְּ עָלִית עַל כֻּלָּנָה.

שֶׁקֶר הַחֵן וְהֶבֶל הַיֹּפִי, אִשָּׁה יִרְאַת יְיָ הִיא תִתְהַלָּל.

תְּנוּ לָהּ מִפְּרִי יָדֶיהָ, וִיהַלְלוּהָ בַשְּׁעָרִים מַעֲשֶׂיהָ.

G'malat'hu tov v'lo rah, kol y'mei hayehah.
Darshah tzemer ufishtim, vata'as b'hefetz kapehah.
Hay'tah k'oniyot soher, mimerhak tavi lahmah.
Vatakom b'od lylah, vatiten teref l'veitah v'hok l'na'arotehah.
Zam'mah sadeh vatikahehu, mipri khapehah nat'ah karem.
Hagrah v'oz motnehah, vat'ametz z'ro-otehah.
Ta'amah ki tov sahrah, lo yikhbeh valahy'lah neirah.
Yadehah shilhah vakishor, v'khapehah tamkhu falekh.
Kapah parsah le'ani, v'yadehah shilhah la'evyon.
Lo tirah l'veitah mishaleg, ki khol beitah lavush shanim.
Marvadim astah lah, sheish v'argaman l'vushah.
Noda bash'arim balah, b'shivto im ziknei aretz.
Sadin astah vatimkor, vahagor natnah lakna'ani.
Oz v'hadar l'vushah, vatishak l'yom aharon.
Pihah pathah v'hokhmah, v'torat hesed al l'shonah.
Tzofiyah halikhot beitah, v'lehem atzlut lo tokhel.
Kamu vanehah va-y'ashruhah, balah v'y'hal'lah.
Rabot banot asu hayil, v'at alit al kulanah.
Sheker hahein v'hevel ha-yofi, ishah yir'at Adonai he tit'halal.
T'nu lah mipri yadehah, vihal'luhah vash'arim ma'asehah.

Proverbs 31:10-13

She does him good and not harm, all the days of her life.

She seeks out wool and flax, and uses her hands to work with them.

She is like a merchant fleet, bringing her food from far away.

She wakes up while it is still night, supplies provisions for her household,
And the daily fare of her maids.

She examines an estate and buys it;
She plants a vineyard by her hard work.

She is very strong and uses her arms for labor.

Her good judgment makes her business successful;
She works very long hours so that her lamp does not go out at night.

She uses her hands on the spinning wheel,
Her palms support the spindle.

She is generous to the poor and extends her hands to the needy.

She does not worry for her household because of snow,
For everyone in her household wears crimson garments.

She makes warm covers for herself;
Her clothing is made of linen and purple cloth like royalty.

Her husband is respected in the council,
As he sits with elders of the land.

She makes cloth and sells it, and offers a belt to the merchant.

She is clothed with strength and luxury;
She looks to the future cheerfully.

She speaks words of wisdom and *Torah* of kindness.

She oversees her household and never eats the bread of idleness.

Her children rise to honor her; her husband praises her.

"Many women have shown valor, but you are exceptional."

If a person is only concerned with grace and beauty that will not last;
A woman filled with awe for *Adonai* will be praised.

Give her credit for the fruit of her hands,
And in the city gates let her works praise her.

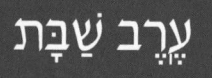

אַשְׁרֵי הָאִישׁ

Ashrei Ha'ish

Happy Is The Man

Ashrei Ha'ish is an egalitarian response to parallel the recitation of *Eishet Hayil*. Both prayers speak of the love, devotion, and commitment couples share. It is customarily recited by a wife to her husband.

הַלְלוּ יָהּ׃
אַשְׁרֵי־אִישׁ יָרֵא אֶת־יְיָ,
בְּמִצְוֹתָיו חָפֵץ מְאֹד.

Hal'lu Yah.
Ashrei ish yareh et Adonai, b'mitzvotav hafetz m'od.

גִּבּוֹר בָּאָרֶץ יִהְיֶה זַרְעוֹ, דּוֹר יְשָׁרִים יְבֹרָךְ.
הוֹן־וָעֹשֶׁר בְּבֵיתוֹ, וְצִדְקָתוֹ עֹמֶדֶת לָעַד.
זָרַח בַּחֹשֶׁךְ אוֹר לַיְשָׁרִים, חַנּוּן וְרַחוּם וְצַדִּיק....
מִשְּׁמוּעָה רָעָה לֹא יִירָא, נָכוֹן לִבּוֹ בָּטֻחַ בַּיְיָ.
סָמוּךְ לִבּוֹ לֹא יִירָא....
פִּזַּר נָתַן לָאֶבְיוֹנִים צִדְקָתוֹ עֹמֶדֶת לָעַד,
קַרְנוֹ תָּרוּם בְּכָבוֹד....

Verses from Psalm 112

Gibor ba'aretz yihyeh zar'o, dor y'sharim y'vorakh.
Hon va'osher b'veito, v'tzidkato omedet la'ad.
Zarah bahoshekh or la-y'sharim, hanun v'rahum v'tzadik.
Mishmu'ah ra'ah lo yira, nakhon libo batuah b'Adonai.
Samukh libo lo yira....
Pizar natan la'evyonim tzidkato omedet la'ad,
karno tarum b'khavod....

Blessed is the man who honors *Adonai,*
He finds joy in observing God's commandments.
His descendants will be mighty in the land,
A blessed generation of righteous people.
Wealth/comfort is in his house, and his just behavior lasts forever.
Light shines for the righteous in the darkness,
For he is gracious, compassionate, and just....
He is not afraid of evil news, his heart is firm, trusting in *Adonai.*
His heart is steady, he is not afraid....
He generously gives *tz'dakah* to the poor, his righteousness lasts forever,
His life is honored for his good deeds....

קִדּוּשׁ לְלֵיל שַׁבָּת

Kiddush L'Leil Shabbat

Kiddush for *Shabbat* Evening

The blessing over wine or grape juice helps us rejoice on *Shabbat*, this day that *Adonai* created as holy and special. We fill our glass to the brim symbolizing our overflowing gratitude to God for this weekly gift of rest, renewal, and reflection.

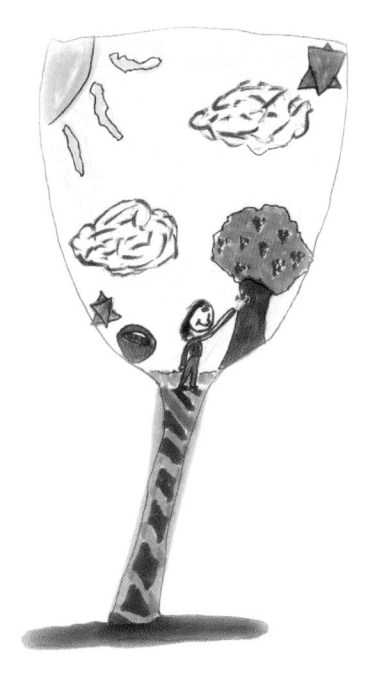

וַיְהִי עֶרֶב וַיְהִי בֹקֶר יוֹם הַשִּׁשִּׁי.
וַיְכֻלּוּ הַשָּׁמַיִם וְהָאָרֶץ וְכָל־צְבָאָם.
וַיְכַל אֱלֹהִים בַּיּוֹם הַשְּׁבִיעִי,
מְלַאכְתּוֹ אֲשֶׁר עָשָׂה,
וַיִּשְׁבֹּת בַּיּוֹם הַשְּׁבִיעִי,
מִכָּל מְלַאכְתּוֹ אֲשֶׁר עָשָׂה.
וַיְבָרֶךְ אֱלֹהִים אֶת יוֹם הַשְּׁבִיעִי,
וַיְקַדֵּשׁ אֹתוֹ, כִּי בוֹ שָׁבַת
מִכָּל מְלַאכְתּוֹ,
אֲשֶׁר בָּרָא אֱלֹהִים לַעֲשׂוֹת.

Genesis 1:31-2:3

סַבְרִי חֲבֵרַי:

בָּרוּךְ אַתָּה יְיָ אֱלֹהֵינוּ מֶלֶךְ הָעוֹלָם,
בּוֹרֵא פְּרִי הַגָּפֶן.

בָּרוּךְ אַתָּה יְיָ אֱלֹהֵינוּ מֶלֶךְ הָעוֹלָם,
אֲשֶׁר קִדְּשָׁנוּ בְּמִצְוֹתָיו וְרָצָה בָנוּ,
וְשַׁבַּת קָדְשׁוֹ בְּאַהֲבָה וּבְרָצוֹן הִנְחִילָנוּ
זִכָּרוֹן לְמַעֲשֵׂה בְרֵאשִׁית,
כִּי הוּא יוֹם תְּחִלָּה לְמִקְרָאֵי קֹדֶשׁ,
זֵכֶר לִיצִיאַת מִצְרָיִם.
כִּי בָנוּ בָחַרְתָּ וְאוֹתָנוּ קִדַּשְׁתָּ מִכָּל הָעַמִּים,
וְשַׁבַּת קָדְשְׁךָ בְּאַהֲבָה וּבְרָצוֹן הִנְחַלְתָּנוּ.
בָּרוּךְ אַתָּה יְיָ מְקַדֵּשׁ הַשַּׁבָּת.

Va'y'hi erev vay'hi voker yom hashishi. Vay'khulu hashamayim v'ha'aretz v'khol tz'va'am. Va'y'khal Elohim bayom hashvi'i, m'lakhto asher asah, vayishbot bayom hashvi'i, mikol m'lakhto asher asah. Va'y'varekh Elohim et yom hashvi'i, va'y'kadesh oto, ki vo shavat mikol m'lakhto, asher barah Elohim la'asot.

Savri <u>h</u>aveirai:
Barukh atah Adonai Eloheinu melekh ha'olam, borei p'ri hagafen.

Barukh atah Adonai, Eloheinu melekh ha'olam, asher kid'shanu b'mitzvotav v'ratzah vanu, v'Shabbat kodsho b'ahava uvratzon hin<u>h</u>ilanu zikaron l'ma'aseh v'reishit, ki hu yom t'<u>h</u>ilah l'mikra'ei kodesh, zekher litzi'at mitzrayim. Ki vanu va<u>h</u>artah v'otanu kidashtah mikol ha'amim, v'Shabbat kodsh'khah b'ahavah uvratzon hin<u>h</u>altanu. Barukh atah Adonai, m'kadesh haShabbat.

"And there was evening and there was morning: the sixth day. The heavens and the earth, and all their contents were completed. On the seventh day God completed all the skilled work. God ceased from all God's work. God blessed the seventh day and declared it holy because on that day God rested from all the acts of creation."
Genesis 1:31-2:3

Praised are You, *Adonai*, our God, Ruler of the universe, Creator of the fruit of the vine. Praised are You, *Adonai*, our God, Ruler of the universe, who makes us holy through Your *mitzvot* and who wants us to be Your people; You gave us the holy *Shabbat*, with love and favor, as our inheritance, a remembrance of the work of Creation. *Shabbat* is first among the sacred days, a reminder of the Exodus from Egypt. For You choose us and You sanctify us from all other peoples; You gave us Your holy *Shabbat* with love and favor as our heritage. Praised are You, *Adonai*, who makes *Shabbat* holy.

· How can we bring *Shabbat* holiness and joy into our lives and into our relationships with each other?

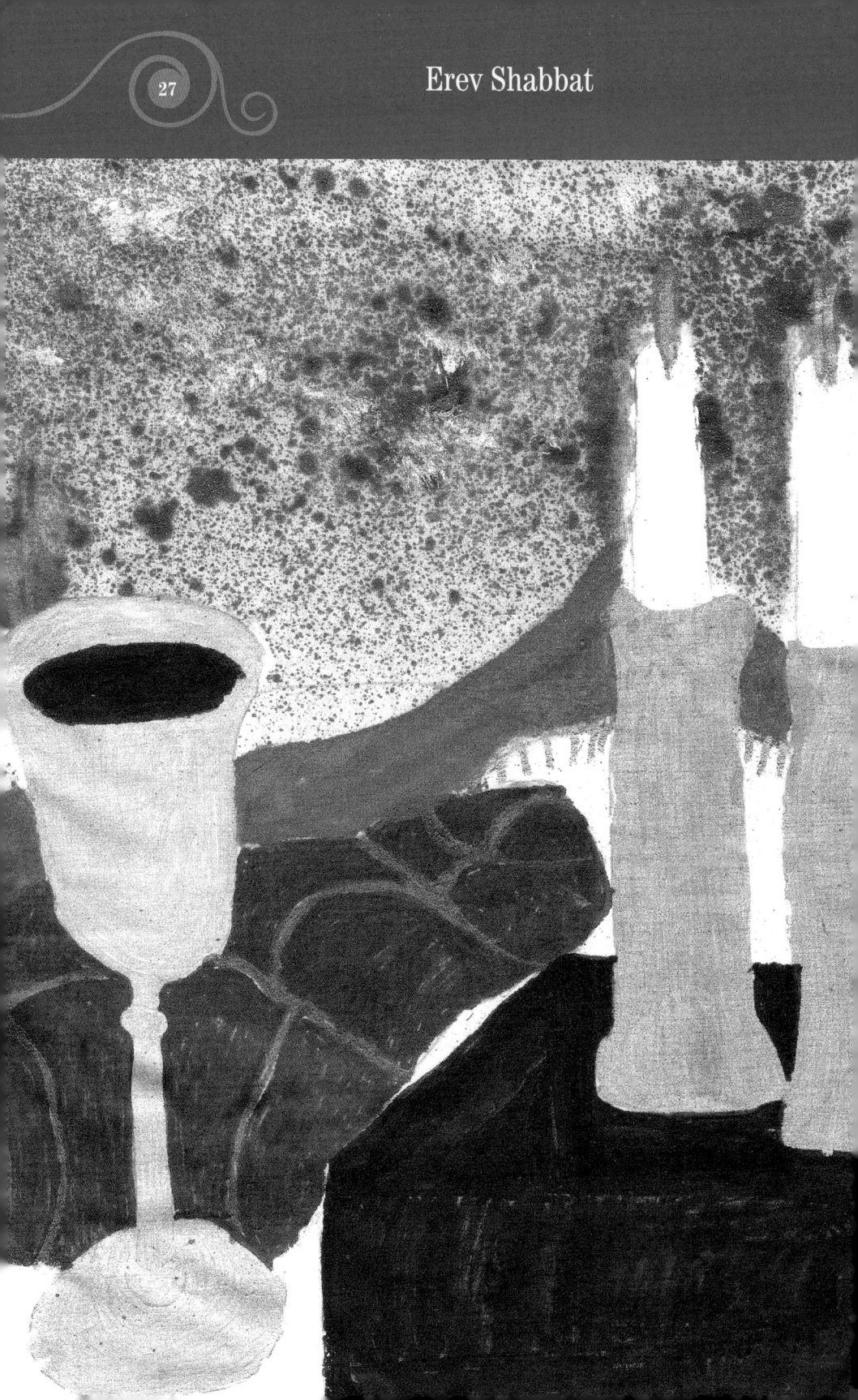

נְטִילַת יָדַיִם

N'tilat Yadayim
Washing Hands

Just as Temple priests washed themselves before offering a sacrifice to God, we purify our hands before eating our *Shabbat* and holiday meals. We use a special cup with two handles and pour warm water on our hands–first left, then right, and afterwards we say the *brakhah*. It is traditional not to speak until we recite *Hamotzi*, (blessing over the meal). This allows us time to focus on God's plentiful gifts before we eat.

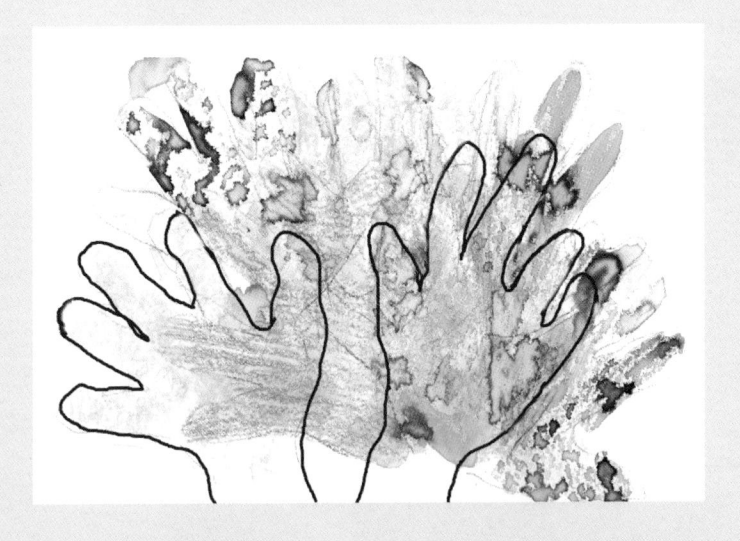

בָּרוּךְ אַתָּה יְיָ אֱלֹהֵינוּ מֶלֶךְ הָעוֹלָם,
אֲשֶׁר קִדְּשָׁנוּ בְּמִצְוֹתָיו וְצִוָּנוּ, עַל נְטִילַת יָדַיִם.

Barukh atah Adonai Eloheinu melekh ha'olam, asher kid'shanu b'mitzvotav v'tzivanu, al n'tilat yadayim.

Praised are You, *Adonai*, our God, Ruler of the universe, who makes us holy through Your *mitzvot*, and commands us to wash our hands.

Hamotzi

הַמוֹצִיא

Blessing Over The Meal

On *Shabbat* and Festivals we share our meal with family and friends. We recite *Hamotzi*, the blessing over two *hallot* reminding us of the double portion of *mannah* that God gave the Israelites every Friday as they wandered in the desert. This extra portion of *mannah* sustained our ancestors when it did not fall from the heavens on *Shabbat*. *Exodus 16*

B'teiyavon — enjoy your delicious meal!

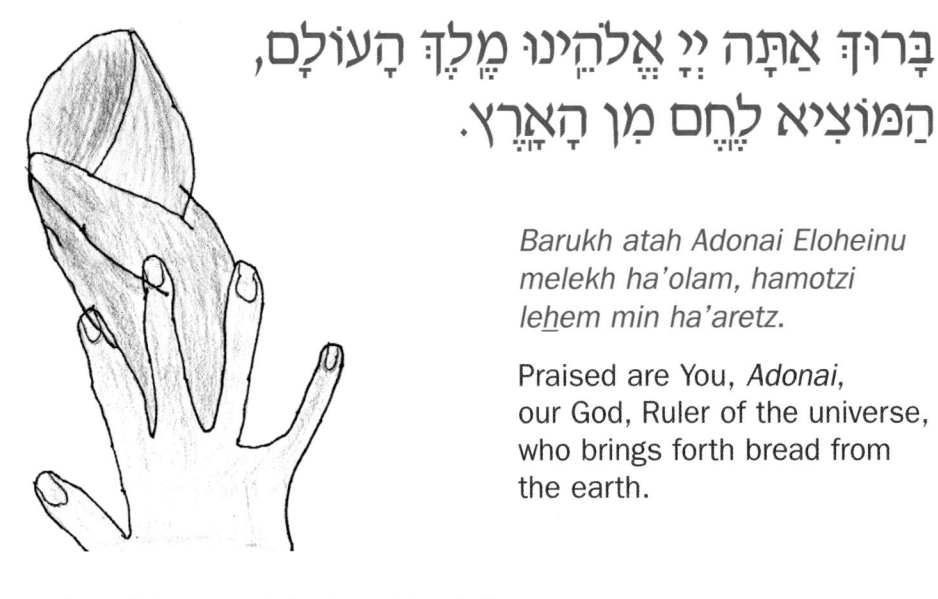

בָּרוּךְ אַתָּה יְיָ אֱלֹהֵינוּ מֶלֶךְ הָעוֹלָם,
הַמוֹצִיא לֶחֶם מִן הָאָרֶץ.

Barukh atah Adonai Eloheinu melekh ha'olam, hamotzi lehem min ha'aretz.

Praised are You, *Adonai*, our God, Ruler of the universe, who brings forth bread from the earth.

· How did *mannah* look and taste?

· How do we show appreciation to God, who created the ingredients for our meal, and the many people involved in bringing it to our table?

· Some people salt their *hallot* to remember that at times of great joy, we think about people less fortunate and work to make their lives better. What are we going to do to help others in the coming week?

לִמּוּד תּוֹרָה
Limud Torah
Torah Study

Enrich your *Shabbat* and Festival celebrations by studying *Parshat Hashavua* (the weekly *Torah* portion) with your family and friends. Our tradition teaches that as children begin to study the *Torah*, their first encounter does not involve books. They do not grapple with difficult texts or explore lofty ideas. Instead, children are offered an *aleph* shaped cookie. As they successfully identify the Hebrew letter, it is then dipped in honey and the children joyfully partake of this sugary treat. Thus we bless our children that their *Torah* study should always be as sweet as honey.

The Rabbis believed in the *Torah's* ability to change every individual. They taught, "As fire leaves a mark on a person's body, so the *Torah* also leaves an impression on a person." *Sifrei Deuteronomy 343*

The Tanya, a Hasidic text, teaches that as bread is absorbed into the body and provides it with sustenance, so too, *Torah* is absorbed by the intellect and sustains the spirit. *Sources and Studies in Kabbalah, Hasidism, and Jewish Thought, Volume 4, The Religious Thought of Hasidism Text and Commentary. Edited by Rabbi Norman Lamm. p. 237.*

We want our learning to penetrate our souls, to be internalized at the deepest levels.

Here are some suggestions to guide your discussions.

• Begin with this *brakhah* for the study of *Torah*:

בָּרוּךְ אַתָּה יְיָ, אֱלֹהֵינוּ מֶלֶךְ הָעוֹלָם,
אֲשֶׁר קִדְּשָׁנוּ בְּמִצְוֹתָיו וְצִוָּנוּ,
לַעֲסֹק בְּדִבְרֵי תוֹרָה.

Barukh atah Adonai Eloheinu melekh ha'olam, asher kid'shanu b'mitzvotav v'tzivanu, la'asok b'divrei Torah.

Praised are You, *Adonai*, Ruler of the universe, who makes us holy through Your *mitzvot* and commands us to study, learn, and teach *Torah*.

- Try to engage in *Torah* study at the same time each week or in advance of *Shabbat* and Festivals. Adults and children in particular, respond favorably and benefit from the predictability of ritual and order. Talking about *Torah* at the table connects us to our children and their school experiences.

- Encourage everyone to participate by reading, speaking, or retelling the *Torah* passage in their own words. Have older children take leadership roles by reading the text in Hebrew or English and leading the discussion.

- Ask a leading question to engage participation and take the conversation to a deeper level. Ask children to share their experiences and reactions. Validate their opinions and answers. Ask follow-up questions,
  "Why do you think this way?"
  "How does it make you feel?"
  "How did Moses or Miriam feel at that moment?"

- Start small when choosing a passage to discuss. Don't be intimidated by the length of any given portion. Wonderful and meaningful discussions occur when studying or discussing one passage or sentence.

- Allow the *Torah* study to be a springboard for other conversations. Do not be worried if you go off in an unexpected direction. End on a positive note and follow up your discussion by referring to it during the week.

Here are some useful _Humashim_ (_Torah_ texts and commentaries) to guide your discussions:

- _Etz Hayim_: _Torah_ and Commentary, senior editor: Rabbi David Lieber. The Rabbinical Assembly and the United Synagogue of Conservative Judaism. 2001.

- _The Stone Edition of the Chumash: The Torah, Haftaros, and Five Megillos with a commentary from Rabbinic writings_, by Rabbi Nosson Scherman. 1994.

- _The Torah: A Modern Commentary_, edited by Rabbi W. Gunther Plaut. Union for Reform Judaism Press. Revised 2005.

- _A Torah Commentary for our Times_, edited by Rabbi Harvey Fields. Union for Reform Judaism Press. 1993.

There are also a variety of family-friendly and easy to read Jewish online learning opportunities to support your study and discussions:

MyJewishLearning.com
This comprehensive website contains information on most Jewish topics and is arranged by levels.

www.urj.org
The Union for Reform Judaism website contains "Weekly Family *Shabbat* Table Talk" to facilitate *Torah* discussions including suggestions on how to engage young children and ideas for creative holiday celebrations.

www.jtsa.edu/community/parashah
The Jewish Theological Seminary of America publishes a weekly *D'var Torah* (words of *Torah*) teaching about the *Torah* portion.

www.ou.org/*shabbat*
The Union of Orthodox Congregations publishes a weekly *D'var Torah.*

www.jrf.org
The Jewish Reconstructionist Foundation publishes a weekly *D'var Torah.*

צֵא וּלְמַד *Tzei ulmad* – the *Talmud* uses this phrase to encourage us to go and study *Torah*. Go, learn, discuss, and enjoy studying *Torah* with your family and friends!

זְמִירוֹת לְשַׁבָּת וּלְיוֹם טוֹב
Z'mirot L'Shabbat ul'Yom Tov
Shabbat and Festival Songs

Choose one or more *z'mirot* (songs) to enhance your *Shabbat* and Festival celebrations, singing a verse or the complete *z'mirah* during and after the meal. The *z'mirot* express our thanks to God for *Shabbat*, Festivals, *Torah*, prayer, and delicious foods.

Al Sh'loshah D'varim

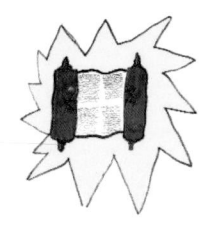

עַל שְׁלֹשָׁה דְבָרִים הָעוֹלָם עוֹמֵד:
עַל הַתּוֹרָה וְעַל הָעֲבוֹדָה
וְעַל גְּמִילוּת חֲסָדִים.

Al shloshah d'varim ha'olam omeid:
al haTorah, v'al ha'avodah v'al g'milut ḥasadim.

The world stands on three things:
The study of *Torah*, prayer to God, and acts of loving kindness.
Pirkei Avot 1:2

Am Yisra'el Ḥai

Am Yisra'el ḥai. Od avinu ḥai.

The Jewish people lives.
Our father (Jacob) still lives.
Genesis 45:3

עַם יִשְׂרָאֵל חָי.
עוֹד אָבִינוּ חָי.

Bim Bam - Shabbat Shalom

Bim bam, bim bim bim bam, bim bim bim bim bim bam. (2) Shabbat Shalom (2), Shabbat (3), Shabbat Shalom.

בִּים בָּם.
שַׁבָּת שָׁלוֹם.

David Melekh Yisra'el

דָּוִד מֶלֶךְ יִשְׂרָאֵל חַי וְקַיָּם.

David, melekh yisra'el, <u>h</u>ai <u>h</u>ai v'kaiyam.

David, King of Israel, lives forever.

Dodi Li

דּוֹדִי לִי וַאֲנִי לוֹ, הָרוֹעֶה בַּשּׁוֹשַׁנִּים.

Dodi li va'ani lo,
haro'eh bashoshanim.

My beloved is mine and I am his,
As a shepherd (who cares for sheep)
among the lilies.

Song of Songs 2:16

Eileh <u>H</u>amdah Libi

אֵלֶּה חָמְדָה לִבִּי
חוּסָה נָא וְאַל נָא תִּתְעַלֵּם.

Eileh <u>h</u>amdah libi,
<u>h</u>usah na v'al na tit'aleim.

These are my heart's desires.
Be compassionate and don't hide
from me.

Eleazar Azikri

Hava Nashirah

הָבָה נָשִׁירָה שִׁיר הַלְלוּיָה.

Havah nashirah shir halleluyah.

Let's sing a song of Halleluyah.

Hineih Mah Tov

הִנֵּה מַה טוֹב וּמַה נָּעִים
שֶׁבֶת אַחִים גַּם יָחַד.

Hineih mah tov u-mah na'im shevet aḥim gam yaḥad.

How wonderful it is for us to be together!

Psalm 133:1

Kol Han'shamah

*Kol han'shamah t'haleil Yah,
Halleluyah!*

Let everyone praise God: *Halleluyah!*

Psalm 150:6

כָּל הַנְּשָׁמָה תְּהַלֵּל יָהּ
הַלְלוּיָהּ.

L'khah Dodi

לְכָה דוֹדִי לִקְרַאת כַּלָּה
פְּנֵי שַׁבָּת נְקַבְּלָה.

שָׁמוֹר וְזָכוֹר בְּדִבּוּר אֶחָד
הִשְׁמִיעָנוּ אֵל הַמְיֻחָד
יְיָ אֶחָד וּשְׁמוֹ אֶחָד
לְשֵׁם וּלְתִפְאֶרֶת וְלִתְהִלָּה.

L'khah dodi likrat kalah p'nei Shabbat n'kablah. Shamor v'zakhor b'dibur ehad hishmi'anu Eil ham'yuhad. Adonai ehad ush'mo ehad l'shem ul'tif'eret v'lithilah.

Come, my friend, to greet the Bride:
Let's welcome the presence of *Shabbat*.

"Guard" and "Remember" (to observe *Shabbat*) were taught in one word, by our God who caused us to hear (the command at Mount Sinai). *Adonai* is One and the Divine name is One, reflected in glory, fame, and praise.   *Rabbi Solomon Alkebetz, Siddur: Friday evening service*

Lo Yisah Goy

לֹא יִשָּׂא גוֹי אֶל גוֹי חֶרֶב
וְלֹא יִלְמְדוּ עוֹד מִלְחָמָה.

Lo yisah goy el goy herev,
V'lo yilm'du od milhamah.

Nation shall not lift up sword against nation. They shall never again learn war. *Isaiah 2:4*

Mah Yafeh Hayom

מַה יָּפֶה הַיּוֹם שַׁבָּת שָׁלוֹם.

Mah yafeh hayom, Shabbat Shalom (2). Shabbat, Shabbat Shalom (3) Shabbat Shalom.

How beautiful is the day! *Shabbat Shalom.*

Yism'ḥu B'malkhut'khah

יִשְׂמְחוּ בְמַלְכוּתְךָ שׁוֹמְרֵי שַׁבָּת,
וְקוֹרְאֵי עֹנֶג שַׁבָּת.

Yism'ḥu b'malkhut'khah shomrei,
Shomrei, shomrei Shabbat,
V'kor'ei oneg Shabbat.

Those who celebrate *Shabbat* rejoice in Your reign and call *Shabbat* a delight.
Siddur: Shabbat Musaf

D'ror Yikrah

דְּרוֹר יִקְרָא לְבֵן עִם בַּת
וְיִנְצָרְכֶם כְּמוֹ בָבַת
נְעִים שִׁמְכֶם וְלֹא יֻשְׁבַּת
שְׁבוּ וְנוּחוּ בְּיוֹם שַׁבָּת.

דְּרוֹשׁ נָוִי וְאוּלַמִּי
וְאוֹת יֶשַׁע עֲשֵׂה עִמִּי
נְטַע שׂוֹרֵק בְּתוֹךְ כַּרְמִי
שְׁעֵה שַׁוְעַת בְּנֵי עַמִּי.

D'ror yikrah l'vein im bat
V'yintzorkhem k'mo vavat.
Ne'im shimkhem v'lo yushbat
Sh'vu v'nu<u>h</u>u b'yom Shabbat.

D'rosh navi v'ulami
V'ot yeshah aseh imi.
N'ta soreik b'tokh karmi
Sh'eih shav'at b'nei ami.

God will proclaim freedom for all God's children
And will guard you as the apple of God's eye
Your name will be pleasing and your fame will not end
Sit down and relax on *Shabbat* day.
(God), seek the comfort of my sanctuary and its entry hall.
Give me a sign that You will bring deliverance.
Plant a vine in my vineyard.
Respond to the cry for help from my people.

Dunash ben Labrat

M'nuḥah V'simḥah

מְנוּחָה וְשִׂמְחָה אוֹר לַיְּהוּדִים,
יוֹם שַׁבָּתוֹן יוֹם מַחֲמַדִּים,
שׁוֹמְרָיו וְזוֹכְרָיו הֵמָּה מְעִידִים,
כִּי לְשִׁשָׁה כֹּל בְּרוּאִים וְעוֹמְדִים.

שְׁמֵי שָׁמַיִם אֶרֶץ וְיַמִּים,
כָּל צְבָא מָרוֹם גְּבוֹהִים וְרָמִים,
תַּנִּין וְאָדָם וְחַיַּת רְאֵמִים,
כִּי בְּיָהּ יְיָ צוּר עוֹלָמִים.

הוּא אֲשֶׁר דִּבֶּר לְעַם סְגֻלָּתוֹ,
שָׁמוֹר לְקַדְּשׁוֹ מִבּוֹאוֹ וְעַד צֵאתוֹ,
שַׁבַּת קֹדֶשׁ יוֹם חֶמְדָּתוֹ,
כִּי בוֹ שָׁבַת אֵל מִכָּל מְלַאכְתּוֹ.

בְּמִצְוַת שַׁבָּת אֵל יַחֲלִיצָךְ,
קוּם קְרָא אֵלָיו יָחִישׁ לְאַמְּצָךְ,
נִשְׁמַת כָּל חַי וְגַם נַעֲרִיצָךְ,
אֱכוֹל בְּשִׂמְחָה כִּי כְבָר רָצָךְ.

M'nuḥah v'simḥah or la-y'hudim,
Yom Shabbaton yom maḥamadim,
Shomrav v'zokhrav heimah m'idim,
Ki l'shishah kol b'ru'im ve'omdim.

Sh'mei shamayim eretz v'yamim,
Kol tz'va marom g'vohim v'ramim,
Tanin v'adam v'ḥayat r'eimim,
Ki b'yah Adonai tzur olamim.

Hu asher diber l'am s'gulato,
Shamor l'kad'sho mibo'o v'ad tzeito,
Shabbat kodesh yom ḥemdato,
Ki vo shavat Eil mikol m'lakhto.

B'mitzvat Shabbat Eil yaḥalitzakh,
Kum k'rah eilav yaḥish l'amtzakh,
Nishmat kol ḥai v'gam na'aritzakh,
Ekhol b'simḥah ki kh'var ratzakh.

Rest and joy is the "light for the Jews."
Shabbat day is the divine day of delight.
Those who "keep" it and "remember" it witness that
At the end of the six days,
Everything was created and in place.

The sky, the earth and the seas,
All the heavenly bodies, high above,
The sea-monster, the human and even the great wild ox.
Yet, we trust in *Adonai*, the Rock without end.

God told the treasured people:
"Keep *Shabbat* and sanctify it" *Deuteronomy 5:12*
From its start until its end.
Shabbat is holy, a day of delights,
"For on that day God ceased
From all God's labor." *Genesis 2:3*

God will strengthen and reward you
For observing the *mitzvah* of *Shabbat*.
So get up (early) to pray to God
And God will quickly grant you courage,
(Sing the *Shabbat* morning prayers) *Nishmat* and *Na'aritzkha*,
Go, "eat with joy...for God approved your action long ago."
Ecclesiastes 9:7

Moshe was an anonymous medieval poet whose name appears as an acrostic in the first three stanzas.

Tzur Mishelo Akhalnu

צוּר מִשֶּׁלּוֹ אָכַלְנוּ בָּרְכוּ אֱמוּנַי,
שָׂבַעְנוּ וְהוֹתַרְנוּ כִּדְבַר יְיָ.

הַזָּן אֶת עוֹלָמוֹ רוֹעֵנוּ אָבִינוּ,
אָכַלְנוּ אֶת לַחְמוֹ וְיֵינוֹ שָׁתִינוּ,
עַל כֵּן נוֹדֶה לִשְׁמוֹ
וּנְהַלְלוֹ בְּפִינוּ,
אָמַרְנוּ וְעָנִינוּ אֵין קָדוֹשׁ כַּיְיָ.
צוּר מִשֶּׁלּוֹ אָכַלְנוּ....

בְּשִׁיר וְקוֹל תּוֹדָה נְבָרֵךְ לֵאלֹהֵינוּ,
עַל אֶרֶץ חֶמְדָּה טוֹבָה שֶׁהִנְחִיל לַאֲבוֹתֵינוּ,
מָזוֹן וְצֵדָה הִשְׂבִּיעַ לְנַפְשֵׁנוּ,
חַסְדּוֹ גָּבַר עָלֵינוּ וֶאֱמֶת יְיָ.   צוּר מִשֶּׁלּוֹ אָכַלְנוּ....

Tzur mishelo akhalnu bar'khu emunai, savanu v'hotarnu kidvar Adonai.

Hazan et olamo ro'einu avinu,
Akhalnu et lahmo v'yeino shatinu,
Al kein nodeh lishmo unhal'lo b'finu,
Amarnu v'aninu ein kadosh k'Adonai.
Tzur mishelo....

B'shir v'kol todah n'varekh l'Eloheinu,
Al eretz hemdah tovah, shehinhil la'avoteinu,
Mazon v'tzeida hisbia l'nafsheinu,
Hasdo gavar aleinu v'emet Adonai.
Tzur mishelo....

Let us, my faithful friends, bless the Divine Rock
Whose food we have eaten.
We have eaten our fill and even have food left over as God promised.

The Provider of food for the world is our Shepherd and our Parent,
We have eaten God's bread and drunk God's wine,
Let's acknowledge the Divine name and praise God,
We sing: "There is no one as holy as *Adonai*."

Hannah, the prophet Samuel's mother, I Samuel 2:2

We bless God with song for the good land
That God gave to our ancestors as an inheritance,
With food, God filled our souls,
God's kindness overwhelms us, *Adonai* is true and reliable.

בִּרְכַּת הַמָּזוֹן

Birkat Hamazon

Blessing After Meals

The *mitzvah* of saying a formal "thank you" after we eat developed from these words in Deuteronomy 8:10: "When you have eaten your fill, give thanks to *Adonai* your God for the good land which God has given you." In *Birkat Hamazon* we express our gratitude to God for the delicious food and to those who prepared our meal. We are grateful to God for the land of Israel and work for Messianic times when everyone will eat their fill and hunger will be no more. We begin with the ancient Pilgrim's song.   *Psalm 126*

שִׁיר הַמַּעֲלוֹת.

בְּשׁוּב יְיָ אֶת שִׁיבַת צִיּוֹן הָיִינוּ כְּחֹלְמִים.

אָז יִמָּלֵא שְׂחוֹק פִּינוּ וּלְשׁוֹנֵנוּ רִנָּה.

אָז יֹאמְרוּ בַגּוֹיִם הִגְדִּיל יְיָ לַעֲשׂוֹת עִם אֵלֶּה.

הִגְדִּיל יְיָ לַעֲשׂוֹת עִמָּנוּ, הָיִינוּ שְׂמֵחִים.

שׁוּבָה יְיָ אֶת שְׁבִיתֵנוּ כַּאֲפִיקִים בַּנֶּגֶב.

הַזֹּרְעִים בְּדִמְעָה, בְּרִנָּה יִקְצֹרוּ.

הָלוֹךְ יֵלֵךְ וּבָכֹה, נֹשֵׂא מֶשֶׁךְ הַזָּרַע,

בֹּא יָבֹא בְרִנָּה, נֹשֵׂא אֲלֻמֹּתָיו.

Shir hama'lot: B'shuv Adonai et shivat tziyon hayinu k'holmim.
Az yimaleih s'hok pinu ulshoneinu rinah.
Az yomru vagoyim: "Higdil Adonai la'asot im eileh."
Higdil Adonai la'asot imanu, hayinu s'meihim.
Shuvah Adonai et sh'viteinu ka'afikim ba'Negev.
Hazor'im b'dim'ah b'rinah yiktzoru.
Halokh yeileikh uvakho, noseih meshekh hazara,
Bo yavo v'rinah, nosei alumotav.

A Pilgrim song. When *Adonai* restored the fortunes of Zion, we were as in a dream. Then we laughed and sang songs of joy. Other nations will say: '*Adonai* did great things for them.' *Adonai* will do great things for us and we will be happy. *Adonai* will restore our fortune such as giving us streams of water in the Negev desert. The farmers who cried when they planted, will joyously celebrate their harvest in song. One who walks and weeps due to carrying a heavy sack of seeds—will come home in joy bringing sheaves of grain.

Zimun (invitation for a group). For those praying alone begin on page 47.

Leader:

חֲבֵרַי נְבָרֵךְ.

Haveirai n'varekh.

All:

יְהִי שֵׁם יְיָ מְבֹרָךְ מֵעַתָּה וְעַד עוֹלָם.

Y'hi sheim Adonai m'vorakh mei'atah v'ad olam.

Leader:

יְהִי שֵׁם יְיָ מְבֹרָךְ מֵעַתָּה וְעַד עוֹלָם.

בִּרְשׁוּת חֲבֵרַי, נְבָרֵךְ (אֱלֹהֵינוּ) שֶׁאָכַלְנוּ מִשֶּׁלוֹ.

Y'hi sheim Adonai m'vorakh mei'atah v'ad olam.
Bir'shut haveirai, n'varekh (with 10 people add Eloheinu)
she'akhalnu mishelo.

All:

בָּרוּךְ (אֱלֹהֵינוּ) שֶׁאָכַלְנוּ מִשֶּׁלוֹ וּבְטוּבוֹ חָיִינוּ.

Barukh (Eloheinu) she'akhalnu mishelo uv'tuvo hayinu.

Leader:

בָּרוּךְ (אֱלֹהֵינוּ) שֶׁאָכַלְנוּ מִשֶּׁלוֹ וּבְטוּבוֹ חָיִינוּ.

Barukh (Eloheinu) she'akhalnu mishelo uv'tuvo hayinu.

All:

בָּרוּךְ הוּא וּבָרוּךְ שְׁמוֹ.

Barukh hu uvarukh sh'mo.

My friends, let us bless.
May *Adonai's* name be praised now and forever.
May *Adonai's* name be praised now and forever. With your
permission, let us bless (our God) whose food we have eaten.
Praised is (our God) whose food we have eaten
and by whose goodness we live.
Praised is (our God) whose food we have eaten
and by whose goodness we live.
Praised be God and praised be God's name.
(For the complete version of *Birkat Hamazon* turn to page 52)

בָּרוּךְ אַתָּה יְיָ, אֱלֹהֵינוּ מֶלֶךְ הָעוֹלָם,
הַזָּן אֶת הָעוֹלָם כֻּלּוֹ בְּטוּבוֹ, בְּחֵן בְּחֶסֶד
וּבְרַחֲמִים. הוּא נוֹתֵן לֶחֶם לְכָל-בָּשָׂר, כִּי
לְעוֹלָם חַסְדּוֹ. וּבְטוּבוֹ הַגָּדוֹל תָּמִיד לֹא חָסַר
לָנוּ, וְאַל יֶחְסַר לָנוּ מָזוֹן לְעוֹלָם וָעֶד, בַּעֲבוּר
שְׁמוֹ הַגָּדוֹל, כִּי הוּא אֵל זָן וּמְפַרְנֵס לַכֹּל,
וּמֵיטִיב לַכֹּל, וּמֵכִין מָזוֹן לְכָל-בְּרִיּוֹתָיו אֲשֶׁר
בָּרָא. בָּרוּךְ אַתָּה יְיָ, הַזָּן אֶת הַכֹּל.

Barukh atah Adonai Eloheinu melekh ha'olam,
hazan et ha'olam kulo b'tuvo, b'hein, b'hesed uv'rahamim.
Hu notein lehem l'khol basar, ki l'olamhasdo. Uv'tuvo
hagadol tamid lo hasar lanu, v'al yehsar lanu mazon l'olam
va'ed, ba'avur sh'mo hagadol. Ki hu Eil zan um'farneis lakol,
umeitiv lakol, umeikhin mazon l'khol b'riyotav asher barah.
Barukh atah Adonai, hazan et hakol.

Praised are You, *Adonai*, our God, Ruler of the universe, who feeds
the world with goodness, graciousness, love, and compassion. God
provides food to every creature for God's love endures forever.

God's great goodness has never
failed us. May God's great glory
always assure us food. God feeds,
provides, does good, and prepares
food for all of God's creatures.
Praised are You, *Adonai*, Provider
of food for all.

נוֹדֶה לְךָ יְיָ אֱלֹהֵינוּ, עַל שֶׁהִנְחַלְתָּ לַאֲבוֹתֵינוּ
וּלְאִמּוֹתֵינוּ אֶרֶץ חֶמְדָּה טוֹבָה וּרְחָבָה,
בְּרִית וְתוֹרָה, חַיִּים וּמָזוֹן.
יִתְבָּרַךְ שִׁמְךָ בְּפִי כָל חַי
תָּמִיד לְעוֹלָם וָעֶד,
כַּכָּתוּב: וְאָכַלְתָּ וְשָׂבֶעְתָּ
וּבֵרַכְתָּ אֶת יְיָ אֱלֹהֶיךָ
עַל הָאָרֶץ הַטּוֹבָה
אֲשֶׁר נָתַן לָךְ.
בָּרוּךְ אַתָּה יְיָ,
עַל הָאָרֶץ וְעַל הַמָּזוֹן.

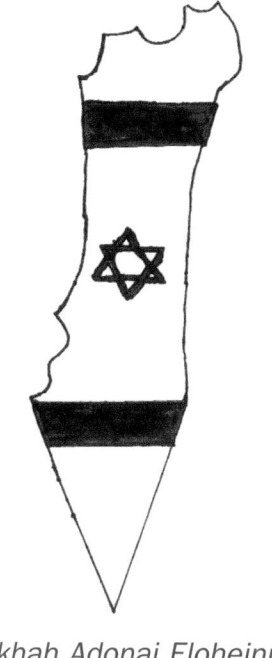

Nodeh l'khah Adonai Eloheinu, al shehinhaltah la'avoteinu
ul'imoteinu eretz hemdah tovah ur'havah, b'rit v'Torah,
hayim umazon. Yitbarakh shimkhah b'fi khol-hai tamid
l'olam va'ed, Kakatuv: "v'akhaltah v'savatah uverakhtah
et-Adonai Elohekha al ha'aretz hatovah asher natan lakh."
Barukh atah Adonai, al ha'aretz v'al hamazon.

We thank You, *Adonai* our God, for giving a lovely and spacious land
to our ancestors as a heritage, the covenant and the *Torah*, life and
food. Your name shall forever be praised by every living being. The
Torah teaches: "And when you have eaten, and are satisfied, you
shall praise *Adonai*, your God, for the good land God gave you."

Deuteronomy 8:10

Praised are You, *Adonai*, for the land and for the food.

וּבְנֵה יְרוּשָׁלַיִם עִיר הַקֹּדֶשׁ בִּמְהֵרָה בְיָמֵינוּ.
בָּרוּךְ אַתָּה יְיָ, בּוֹנֵה בְּרַחֲמָיו יְרוּשָׁלָיִם. אָמֵן.

Uv'nei Y'rushalayim
ir hakodesh bim'heirah
v'yameinu. Barukh atah
Adonai, boneh v'rahamav
Y'rushalayim. Amein.

May God rebuild Jerusalem,
the Holy City, soon, and in our
days. Praised are You, *Adonai*,
who with compassion rebuilds
Jerusalem. Amen.

בָּרוּךְ אַתָּה יְיָ, אֱלֹהֵינוּ מֶלֶךְ הָעוֹלָם,
הַמֶּלֶךְ הַטּוֹב וְהַמֵּיטִיב לַכֹּל. הוּא הֵיטִיב,
הוּא מֵיטִיב, הוּא יֵיטִיב לָנוּ. הוּא גְמָלָנוּ,
הוּא גוֹמְלֵנוּ, הוּא יִגְמְלֵנוּ לָעַד, חֵן וָחֶסֶד
וְרַחֲמִים, וִיזַכֵּנוּ לִימוֹת הַמָּשִׁיחַ.

*Barukh atah Adonai, Eloheinu melekh ha'olam, hamelekh
hatov v'hameitiv lakol. Hu heitiv, hu meitiv, hu yeitiv lanu.
Hu g'malanu, hu gomleinu, hu yig'm'leinu la'ad, hein vahesed
v'rahamim, vizakeinu limot HaMashiah.*

Praised are You, *Adonai*, our God, Ruler of the universe, who is
good and does good for all. God has, is, and will be good to us.
God gave, gives, and will give us forever, grace, kindness,
compassion, and allow us to experience the days of the Messiah.

Shabbat:

הָרַחֲמָן הוּא יַנְחִילֵנוּ יוֹם שֶׁכֻּלּוֹ שַׁבָּת,
וּמְנוּחָה לְחַיֵּי הָעוֹלָמִים.

*Harahaman hu yanhileinu yom shekulo Shabbat,
um'nuhah l'hayei ha'olamim.*

May the Merciful One give us a day that is completely *Shabbat*, and eternal rest in the world to come.

Festivals:

הָרַחֲמָן הוּא יַנְחִילֵנוּ יוֹם שֶׁכֻּלּוֹ טוֹב.

Harahaman hu yanhileinu yom shekulo tov.

May the Merciful One give us a day that will be entirely good.

וְנִשָּׂא בְרָכָה מֵאֵת יְיָ, וּצְדָקָה מֵאֱלֹהֵי יִשְׁעֵנוּ,
וְנִמְצָא חֵן וְשֵׂכֶל טוֹב בְּעֵינֵי אֱלֹהִים וְאָדָם.
עוֹשֶׂה שָׁלוֹם בִּמְרוֹמָיו, הוּא יַעֲשֶׂה שָׁלוֹם
עָלֵינוּ וְעַל כָּל-יִשְׂרָאֵל, וְאִמְרוּ אָמֵן.

*V'nisah v'rakhah me'eit Adonai, utz'dakah mei'Elohei
yish'einu. V'nimtzah hein v'seikhel tov b'einei Elohim v'adam.
Oseh shalom bimromav, hu ya'aseh shalom aleinu v'al kol
Yisra'eil, v'imru Amein.*

May we receive a blessing from *Adonai* and justice from God who saves us. May we find grace and favor from God and people. May God who creates peace, create peace for us, for all Israel, for everyone on earth, and let us say, Amen.

בִּרְכַּת הַמָּזוֹן

Birkat Hamazon

Blessing After Meals

The complete version begins with *Shir Hama'alot* and *Zimun* on pages 44-46 and continues here:

בָּרוּךְ אַתָּה יְיָ אֱלֹהֵינוּ מֶלֶךְ הָעוֹלָם, הַזָּן אֶת הָעוֹלָם כֻּלּוֹ בְּטוּבוֹ, בְּחֵן, בְּחֶסֶד וּבְרַחֲמִים. הוּא נוֹתֵן לֶחֶם לְכָל בָּשָׂר, כִּי לְעוֹלָם חַסְדּוֹ. וּבְטוּבוֹ הַגָּדוֹל תָּמִיד לֹא חָסַר לָנוּ, וְאַל יֶחְסַר לָנוּ מָזוֹן לְעוֹלָם וָעֶד, בַּעֲבוּר שְׁמוֹ הַגָּדוֹל. כִּי הוּא אֵל זָן וּמְפַרְנֵס לַכֹּל, וּמֵטִיב לַכֹּל וּמֵכִין מָזוֹן לְכָל בְּרִיּוֹתָיו אֲשֶׁר בָּרָא. בָּרוּךְ אַתָּה יְיָ, הַזָּן אֶת הַכֹּל.

Barukh atah Adonai Eloheinu melekh ha'olam, hazan et ha'olam kulo b'tuvo, b'hein, b'hesed uv'rahamim. Hu notein lehem l'khol basar, ki l'olam hasdo. Uv'tuvo hagadol tamid lo hasar lanu, v'al yehsar lanu mazon l'olam va'ed, ba'avur sh'mo hagadol. Ki hu Eil zan um'farneis lakol, umeitiv lakol umeikhin mazon l'khol bri'yotav asher barah. Barukh atah Adonai, hazan et hakol.

Praised are You, *Adonai*, our God, Ruler of the universe, who feeds the world with goodness, graciousness, love, and compassion. God provides food to every creature for God's love endures forever. God's great goodness has never failed us. May God's great glory always assure us food. God feeds, provides, does good, and prepares food for all of God's creatures. Praised are You, *Adonai*, Provider of food for all.

נוֹדֶה לְּךָ יְיָ אֱלֹהֵינוּ עַל שֶׁהִנְחַלְתָּ לַאֲבוֹתֵינוּ
וּלְאִמוֹתֵינוּ, אֶרֶץ חֶמְדָּה טוֹבָה וּרְחָבָה, וְעַל
שֶׁהוֹצֵאתָנוּ יְיָ אֱלֹהֵינוּ מֵאֶרֶץ מִצְרַיִם, וּפְדִיתָנוּ
מִבֵּית עֲבָדִים, וְעַל בְּרִיתְךָ שֶׁחָתַמְתָּ בִּבְשָׂרֵנוּ,
וְעַל תּוֹרָתְךָ שֶׁלִּמַּדְתָּנוּ, וְעַל חֻקֶּיךָ שֶׁהוֹדַעְתָּנוּ,
וְעַל חַיִּים חֵן וָחֶסֶד שֶׁחוֹנַנְתָּנוּ, וְעַל אֲכִילַת
מָזוֹן שָׁאַתָּה זָן וּמְפַרְנֵס אוֹתָנוּ תָּמִיד, בְּכָל יוֹם
וּבְכָל עֵת וּבְכָל שָׁעָה.

*Nodeh l'kha Adonai Eloheinu al shehinhaltah la'avoteinu
ul'imoteinu, eretz hemdah tovah urhavah, v'al shehotzeitanu
Adonai Eloheinu mei'eretz mitzrayim, uf'ditanu mibeit
avadim, v'al britkhah shehatamtah bivsareinu, v'al
Toratkhah shelimad'tanu, v'al hukekhah shehodatanu, v'al
hayim hein vahesed shehonantanu, v'al akhilat mazon
she'atah zan um'farneis otanu tamid, b'khol yom uvkhol eit
uv'khol sha'ah.*

We thank You, *Adonai* our God, for giving a lovely and spacious land
to our ancestors as a heritage, for liberating us from the land of
Egypt and freeing us from the house of bondage. We thank You for
the covenant sealed in our flesh; for teaching us Your *Torah* and Your
laws, for the gift of life, compassion, and kindness You graciously give
us. Thank You for the food we eat, now and continually, every day,
every season, and all times.

Hanukah:

Al hanisim v'al hapurkan,
v'al hag'vurot, v'al hat'shuot,
v'al hamilhamot she'asitah
la'avoteinu bayamim hahem
bazman hazeh. Bimei Matityahu
ben Yohanan kohein gadol,
Hashmonai uvanav,
k'she'amdah malkhut yavan
harsha'ah al amkhah Yisra'el
l'hashkiham Toratekhah
ul'ha'aviram meihukei
r'tzonekhah, v'atah
b'rahamekhah harabim
amad'tah lahem b'eit tzaratam,
ravtah et rivam, dantah et
dinam, nakamtah et-nikmatam,
masartah giborim b'yad
halashim, v'rabim b'yad m'atim,
utmei'im b'yad t'horim, ursha'im
b'yad tzadikim, v'zeidim b'yad
os'kei toratekhah. Ul'kha asitah
sheim gadol v'kadosh
b'olamekhah, ul'amkhah
Yisra'el asitah t'shu'ah g'dolah
ufurkan k'hayom hazeh.
V'ahar kein ba'u vanekhah
lidvir beitekhah ufinu et
heikhalekhah, v'tiharu et
mikdashekhah, v'hidliku neirot
b'hatzrot kodshekhah, v'kavu
sh'monat y'mei Hanukah eilu
l'hodot ul'haleil l'shimkhah hagadol.

עַל הַנִּסִּים וְעַל הַפֻּרְקָן,
וְעַל הַגְּבוּרוֹת, וְעַל הַתְּשׁוּעוֹת,
וְעַל הַמִּלְחָמוֹת שֶׁעָשִׂיתָ
לַאֲבוֹתֵינוּ בַּיָּמִים הָהֵם בַּזְּמַן
הַזֶּה. בִּימֵי מַתִּתְיָהוּ בֶּן יוֹחָנָן
כֹּהֵן גָּדוֹל, חַשְׁמוֹנַאי וּבָנָיו,
כְּשֶׁעָמְדָה מַלְכוּת יָוָן הָרְשָׁעָה
עַל עַמְּךָ יִשְׂרָאֵל לְהַשְׁכִּיחָם
תּוֹרָתֶךָ וּלְהַעֲבִירָם מֵחֻקֵּי
רְצוֹנֶךָ, וְאַתָּה בְּרַחֲמֶיךָ הָרַבִּים
עָמַדְתָּ לָהֶם בְּעֵת צָרָתָם, רַבְתָּ
אֶת רִיבָם, דַּנְתָּ אֶת דִּינָם,
נָקַמְתָּ אֶת נִקְמָתָם, מָסַרְתָּ
גִּבּוֹרִים בְּיַד חַלָּשִׁים, וְרַבִּים
בְּיַד מְעַטִּים, וּטְמֵאִים בְּיַד
טְהוֹרִים, וּרְשָׁעִים בְּיַד
צַדִּיקִים, וְזֵדִים בְּיַד עוֹסְקֵי
תוֹרָתֶךָ. וּלְךָ עָשִׂיתָ שֵׁם גָּדוֹל
וְקָדוֹשׁ בְּעוֹלָמֶךָ, וּלְעַמְּךָ
יִשְׂרָאֵל עָשִׂיתָ תְּשׁוּעָה גְדוֹלָה
וּפֻרְקָן כְּהַיּוֹם הַזֶּה. וְאַחַר כֵּן
בָּאוּ בָנֶיךָ לִדְבִיר בֵּיתֶךָ, וּפִנּוּ
אֶת הֵיכָלֶךָ, וְטִהֲרוּ אֶת
מִקְדָּשֶׁךָ, וְהִדְלִיקוּ נֵרוֹת
בְּחַצְרוֹת קָדְשֶׁךָ, וְקָבְעוּ
שְׁמוֹנַת יְמֵי חֲנֻכָּה אֵלּוּ,
לְהוֹדוֹת וּלְהַלֵּל לְשִׁמְךָ הַגָּדוֹל.

Thank You, God, for the miracles, the deliverance, the mighty acts and the victories that You did for our ancestors in ancient days at this time of year. In the days of Mattathias son of Johanan, the Hasmonean High Priest, and his sons, the evil Greek kingdom arose to force Israel to forget Your *Torah* and disobey Your laws. You in great mercy stood up for them in time of trouble. You argued their case, You defended them, and You punished the wrongs done against them. You delivered the strong into the hands of the weak, the many to the few, the wicked to the pure of heart, the guilty to the innocent, the arrogant to the those faithful to Your *Torah*. You made a great and holy name for Yourself and brought victory and liberation for Your people Israel to this day. Then Your children came to the Temple's Holy of Holies, purified the sanctuary, lit the lights in Your holy courtyard, and set aside these eight days of *Hanukah* to thank You and praise Your great name.

וְעַל הַכֹּל יְיָ אֱלֹהֵינוּ
אֲנַחְנוּ מוֹדִים לָךְ,
וּמְבָרְכִים אוֹתָךְ, יִתְבָּרַךְ
שִׁמְךָ בְּפִי כָל חַי תָּמִיד
לְעוֹלָם וָעֶד, כַּכָּתוּב:
וְאָכַלְתָּ וְשָׂבָעְתָּ וּבֵרַכְתָּ
אֶת יְיָ אֱלֹהֶיךָ עַל הָאָרֶץ הַטּוֹבָה אֲשֶׁר נָתַן לָךְ.
בָּרוּךְ אַתָּה יְיָ, עַל הָאָרֶץ וְעַל הַמָּזוֹן.

V'al hakol Adonai Eloheinu ana<u>h</u>nu modim lakh um'varkhim otakh, yitbarakh shimkhah b'fi khol <u>h</u>ai tamid l'olam va'ed, kakatuv: v'akhaltah v'sava'tah uverakhtah et Adonai Elohekha al ha'aretz hatovah asher natan lakh. Barukh atah Adonai, al ha'aretz v'al hamazon.

For all these blessings, we thank and praise You, *Adonai* our God. Your name shall forever be praised by every living being. The *Torah* teaches: "And when you have eaten and are satisfied, you shall praise *Adonai* your God for the good land God gave you." *Deuteronomy 8:10*

Praised are You, *Adonai*, for the land and for the food.

רַחֶם נָא יְיָ אֱלֹהֵינוּ, עַל יִשְׂרָאֵל עַמֶּךָ, וְעַל יְרוּשָׁלַיִם עִירֶךָ, וְעַל צִיּוֹן מִשְׁכַּן כְּבוֹדֶךָ, וְעַל מַלְכוּת בֵּית דָּוִד מְשִׁיחֶךָ, וְעַל הַבַּיִת הַגָּדוֹל וְהַקָּדוֹשׁ שֶׁנִּקְרָא שִׁמְךָ עָלָיו. אֱלֹהֵינוּ אָבִינוּ, רְעֵנוּ זוּנֵנוּ פַּרְנְסֵנוּ וְכַלְכְּלֵנוּ, וְהַרְוִיחֵנוּ וְהַרְוַח לָנוּ, יְיָ אֱלֹהֵינוּ, מְהֵרָה מִכָּל צָרוֹתֵינוּ. וְנָא אַל תַּצְרִיכֵנוּ, יְיָ אֱלֹהֵינוּ, לֹא לִידֵי מַתְּנַת בָּשָׂר וָדָם, וְלֹא לִידֵי הַלְוָאָתַם, כִּי אִם לְיָדְךָ הַמְּלֵאָה, הַפְּתוּחָה, הַגְּדוֹשָׁה וְהָרְחָבָה, שֶׁלֹּא נֵבוֹשׁ וְלֹא נִכָּלֵם לְעוֹלָם וָעֶד.

Raheim na Adonai Eloheinu, al Yisra'el amekhah, v'al Y'rushalayim irekhah, v'al Tziyon mishkan k'vodekhah, v'al malkhut beit David m'shihekhah, v'al habayit hagadol v'hakadosh shenikrah shimkhah alav. Eloheinu avinu, r'einu zuneinu parn'seinu v'khalk'leinu, v'harviheinu v'harvah lanu, Adonai Eloheinu, m'heira mikol tzaroteinu. V'na al tatzrikheinu, Adonai Eloheinu, lo lidei matnat basar vadam, v'lo lidei halva'atam, ki im l'yadkhah hamlei'ah, haptuhah, hag'dushah v'harhavah, shelo neivosh v'lo nikalem l'olam va'ed.

Have mercy, *Adonai* our God, with Israel Your people, with Jerusalem Your holy city, with *Zion* the home of Your glory, with the royal House of David, Your messiah, and with the great and holy Temple that is called by Your name. Our God, our Parent, tend and nourish us, sustain and maintain us, and quickly give us relief from all our troubles. Prevent us, please, *Adonai* our God, from needing handouts from people, but may we rely only on Your helping and generous hand so that we may never be humiliated or put to shame.

Shabbat:

רְצֵה וְהַחֲלִיצֵנוּ יְיָ אֱלֹהֵינוּ בְּמִצְוֹתֶיךָ, וּבְמִצְוַת יוֹם הַשְּׁבִיעִי הַשַּׁבָּת הַגָּדוֹל וְהַקָּדוֹשׁ הַזֶּה. כִּי יוֹם זֶה גָּדוֹל וְקָדוֹשׁ הוּא לְפָנֶיךָ, לִשְׁבָּת בּוֹ וְלָנוּחַ בּוֹ בְּאַהֲבָה כְּמִצְוַת רְצוֹנֶךָ וּבִרְצוֹנְךָ הָנִיחַ לָנוּ יְיָ אֱלֹהֵינוּ, שֶׁלֹּא תְהֵא צָרָה וְיָגוֹן וַאֲנָחָה בְּיוֹם מְנוּחָתֵנוּ, וְהַרְאֵנוּ יְיָ אֱלֹהֵינוּ בְּנֶחָמַת צִיּוֹן עִירֶךָ, וּבְבִנְיַן יְרוּשָׁלַיִם עִיר קָדְשֶׁךָ, כִּי אַתָּה הוּא בַּעַל הַיְשׁוּעוֹת וּבַעַל הַנֶּחָמוֹת.

R'tzeih v'hahalitzeinu Adonai Eloheinu b'mitzvotekhah, uvmitzvat yom hash'vi'i haShabbat hagadol v'hakadosh hazeh, ki yom zeh gadol v'kadosh hu l'fanekhah lishbat bo v'lanuah bo b'ahavah k'mitzvat r'tzonekhah, uvir'tzonkhah haniah lanu Adonai Eloheinu, shelo t'heh tzarah v'yagon va'anahah b'yom m'nuhateinu, v'hareinu Adonai Eloheinu b'nehamat Tziyon irekhah, uv'vinyan Y'rushalayim ir kodshekhah, ki atah hu ba'al ha'y'shu'ot uva'al hanehamot.

Strengthen us, *Adonai* our God, with Your *mitzvot*, with the *mitzvah* of this great and holy seventh day, this great and sacred *Shabbat*. It is a great and holy day to be in Your presence, time to rest with love, according to Your will. May it be Your will, *Adonai* our God, to grant that our *Shabbat* rest be free from trouble and sadness. Show us, *Adonai* our God, Zion, Your city, comforted and Jerusalem Your holy city rebuilt, for You bring redemption and comfort.

Rosh Hodesh, Festivals and their Intermediate days:

אֱלֹהֵינוּ וֵאלֹהֵי אֲבוֹתֵינוּ וְאִמּוֹתֵינוּ, יַעֲלֶה וְיָבֹא וְיַגִּיעַ, וְיֵרָאֶה וְיֵרָצֶה וְיִשָּׁמַע, וְיִפָּקֵד וְיִזָּכֵר. זִכְרוֹנֵנוּ וּפִקְדוֹנֵנוּ, וְזִכְרוֹן אֲבוֹתֵינוּ וְאִמּוֹתֵינוּ, וְזִכְרוֹן מָשִׁיחַ בֶּן דָּוִד עַבְדֶּךָ, וְזִכְרוֹן יְרוּשָׁלַיִם עִיר קָדְשֶׁךָ, וְזִכְרוֹן כָּל עַמְּךָ בֵּית יִשְׂרָאֵל, לְפָנֶיךָ לִפְלֵיטָה לְטוֹבָה, לְחֵן וּלְחֶסֶד וּלְרַחֲמִים, לְחַיִּים וּלְשָׁלוֹם בְּיוֹם

Shavuot:	Pesah:	Rosh Hodesh:
חַג הַשָּׁבוּעוֹת הַזֶּה.	חַג הַמַּצוֹת הַזֶּה.	רֹאשׁ הַחֹדֶשׁ הַזֶּה.

Sukkot:	Rosh Hashanah:
חַג הַסֻּכּוֹת הַזֶּה.	הַזִּכָּרוֹן הַזֶּה.

Sh'mini Atzeret and *Simhat Torah:*

הַשְּׁמִינִי חַג הָעֲצֶרֶת הַזֶּה.

זָכְרֵנוּ יְיָ אֱלֹהֵינוּ בּוֹ לְטוֹבָה, וּפָקְדֵנוּ בוֹ לִבְרָכָה, וְהוֹשִׁיעֵנוּ בוֹ לְחַיִּים, וּבִדְבַר יְשׁוּעָה וְרַחֲמִים, חוּס וְחָנֵּנוּ, וְרַחֵם עָלֵינוּ וְהוֹשִׁיעֵנוּ, כִּי אֵלֶיךָ עֵינֵינוּ, כִּי אֵל מֶלֶךְ חַנּוּן וְרַחוּם אָתָּה.

Eloheinu v'Elohei avoteinu v'imoteinu, ya'aleh v'yavo v'yagia,
v'yeira'eh v'yeiratzeh v'yishama, v'yipaked v'yizakher.
Zikhroneinu ufikdoneinu, v'zikhron avoteinu v'imoteinu,
v'zikhron mashiah ben David avdekhah, v'zikhron
Y'rushalayim ir kodshekhah, v'zikhron kol amkhah beit
Yisra'el, l'fanekhah lifleitah l'tovah, l'hein ul'hesed
ul'rahamim, l'hayim ul'shalom b'yom:

Rosh Hodesh:	*Pesah:*	*Shavuot:*
Rosh Hahodesh	*Hag Hamatzot*	*Hag Hashavu'ot*
hazeh.	*hazeh.*	*hazeh.*

Rosh Hashanah:	*Sukkot:*
Hazikaron hazeh.	*Hag Hasukkot hazeh.*

Shimini Atzeret and Simhat Torah:
Hashmini Hag Ha'atzeret hazeh.

Zokhreinu Adonai Eloheinu bo l'tovah, u'fokdeinu vo
livrakhah, v'hoshi'einu vo l'hayim, uvidvar y'shu'ah
v'rahamim, hus v'honeinu v'raheim aleinu v'hoshi'einu,
ki eilekhah eineinu, ki Eil hanun v'rahum atah.

Our God and the God of our ancestors, may these thoughts
rise, enter, arrive, and be seen; may they be wanted, heard,
recorded, and remembered. May You consider us and our
deeds, our ancestors, the Messiah, descendant of David,
Your servant, Jerusalem, Your holy city, Your entire people,
the House of Israel for rescue, goodness, grace, kindness,
and compassion on this day of:

Rosh Hodesh.   (*Passover) the* holiday of *matzot.*   *Shavuot.*

(*Rosh Hashanah)* Rememberance.   *Sukkot.*

(*Sh'mini Atzeret* and *Simhat Torah)*
the eighth day concluding *Sukkot.*

Remember us for good, *Adonai*, our God. Give us blessing and preserve us in life. With a proclamation of redemption and mercy, protect us, grant us peace, compassion, and save us, for we turn our eyes to You, for You are our God, our Ruler, merciful and gracious.

וּבְנֵה יְרוּשָׁלַיִם עִיר הַקֹּדֶשׁ בִּמְהֵרָה בְיָמֵינוּ.
בָּרוּךְ אַתָּה יְיָ, בּוֹנֵה בְרַחֲמָיו יְרוּשָׁלַיִם. אָמֵן.

Uv'neh Y'rushalayim ir hakodesh bim'heirah v'yameinu.
Barukh atah Adonai, boneh v'rahamav Y'rushalayim. Amein.

Rebuild Jerusalem, the Holy City, soon, and in our days. Praised are You, *Adonai*, who with compassion rebuilds Jerusalem. Amen.

בָּרוּךְ אַתָּה יְיָ אֱלֹהֵינוּ מֶלֶךְ הָעוֹלָם,
הָאֵל אָבִינוּ מַלְכֵּנוּ אַדִּירֵנוּ בּוֹרְאֵנוּ גּוֹאֲלֵנוּ
יוֹצְרֵנוּ קְדוֹשֵׁנוּ קְדוֹשׁ יַעֲקֹב, רוֹעֵנוּ רוֹעֵה
יִשְׂרָאֵל, הַמֶּלֶךְ הַטּוֹב וְהַמֵּטִיב לַכֹּל,
שֶׁבְּכָל יוֹם וָיוֹם הוּא הֵטִיב, הוּא מֵטִיב,
הוּא יֵיטִיב לָנוּ. הוּא גְמָלָנוּ, הוּא גוֹמְלֵנוּ,

הוּא יִגְמְלֵנוּ לָעַד, לְחֵן וּלְחֶסֶד וּלְרַחֲמִים,
וּלְרֶוַח, הַצָּלָה וְהַצְלָחָה, בְּרָכָה וִישׁוּעָה,
נֶחָמָה, פַּרְנָסָה וְכַלְכָּלָה, וְרַחֲמִים וְחַיִּים
וְשָׁלוֹם וְכָל טוֹב, וּמִכָּל טוּב לְעוֹלָם אַל
יְחַסְּרֵנוּ.

Barukh atah Adonai, Eloheinu melekh ha'olam, ha'Eil avinu malkeinu adireinu boreinu go'aleinu yotzreinu k'dosheinu k'dosh Ya'akov, ro'einu ro'ei Yisra'el, hamelekh hatov v'hameitiv lakol, sheb'khol yom vayom hu heitiv, hu meitiv, hu yeitiv lanu. Hu g'malanu, hu gomleinu, hu yigm'leinu la'ad, l'hein ulhesed ulrahamim, ulrevah, hatzalah, v'hatzlahah b'rakha vishu'ah, nehamah, parnasah v'khalkalah, v'rahamim v'hayim v'shalom v'khol tov, umikol tuv l'olam al y'hasreinu.

Praised is *Adonai* our God, Ruler of the universe, who is our God, our Parent, our Ruler, our Mighty One, our Creator, our Redeemer, our Maker, the Holy One of Jacob, our Shepherd, the Shepherd of Israel, the generous Ruler who does good to all. Daily, God is good and will be good to us. God rewarded us, rewards us, and will continue to reward us forever. May God continue to bless us with grace, loving kindness, compassion and deliverance, prosperity, redemption and consolation, sustenance and mercy, a life of peace and all goodness. May we never lack any of the good things forever.

הָרַחֲמָן הוּא יִמְלֹךְ עָלֵינוּ לְעוֹלָם וָעֶד.
הָרַחֲמָן הוּא יִתְבָּרַךְ בַּשָּׁמַיִם וּבָאָרֶץ.
הָרַחֲמָן הוּא יִשְׁתַּבַּח לְדוֹר דּוֹרִים, וְיִתְפָּאַר
בָּנוּ לָעַד וּלְנֵצַח נְצָחִים, וְיִתְהַדַּר בָּנוּ לָעַד
וּלְעוֹלְמֵי עוֹלָמִים.
הָרַחֲמָן הוּא יְפַרְנְסֵנוּ בְּכָבוֹד.
הָרַחֲמָן הוּא יִשְׁבֹּר עֻלֵנוּ מֵעַל צַוָּארֵנוּ
וְהוּא יוֹלִיכֵנוּ קוֹמְמִיּוּת לְאַרְצֵנוּ.
הָרַחֲמָן הוּא יִשְׁלַח לָנוּ בְּרָכָה מְרֻבָּה
בַּבַּיִת הַזֶּה וְעַל שֻׁלְחָן זֶה שֶׁאָכַלְנוּ עָלָיו.
הָרַחֲמָן הוּא יִשְׁלַח לָנוּ אֶת אֵלִיָּהוּ הַנָּבִיא
זָכוּר לַטּוֹב, וִיבַשֶּׂר לָנוּ בְּשׂוֹרוֹת טוֹבוֹת
יְשׁוּעוֹת וְנֶחָמוֹת.

Haraḥaman hu yimlokh aleinu l'olam va'ed.
Haraḥaman hu yitbarakh bashamayim uva'aretz.
Haraḥaman hu yishtabaḥ l'dor dorim, v'yitpa'ar banu la'ad
  ul'neitzaḥ n'tzaḥim, v'yit-hadar banu la'ad ul'olmei olamim.
Haraḥaman hu y'farn'seinu b'khavod.
Haraḥaman hu yishbor uleinu mei'al tzavareinu v'hu
  yolikheinu kom'miyut l'artzeinu.
Haraḥaman hu yishlaḥ lanu b'rakhah m'rubah babayit hazeh
  v'al shulḥan zeh she'akhalnu alav.
Haraḥaman hu yishlaḥ lanu et Eliyahu hanavi
  zakhur latov, vivaser lanu b'sorot tovot
  y'shu'ot v'neḥamot.

May the Merciful One reign over us forever.

May the Merciful One be praised in heaven and on earth.

May the Merciful One be praised in all generations; may God be glorified through us to all eternity; may God be honored among us forever.

May the Merciful One grant us an honorable living.

May the Merciful One break the yoke of our oppression and lead us in dignity to our ancient homeland.

May the Merciful One send abundant blessing upon this household and upon this table where we have eaten.

May the Merciful One send Elijah the Prophet to us, and may he bring good tidings of redemption and comfort.

When eating at one's own table:

*Harahaman hu y'vareikh oti
(v'et ishti/ishi v'et zar'i)
otanu v'et kol asher lanu.*

הָרַחֲמָן הוּא יְבָרֵךְ
אוֹתִי (וְאֶת
אִשְׁתִּי/אִישִׁי וְאֶת
זַרְעִי) אוֹתָנוּ וְאֶת כָּל
אֲשֶׁר לָנוּ.

May the Merciful One bless me,
(my wife/husband, my children)
and all my family,

When eating at one's parents' table:

*Harahaman hu y'vareikh et
avi mori ba'al habayit
hazeh, v'et imi morati
ba'alat habayit hazeh,
otam v'et beitam v'et
zar'am v'et kol asher
lahem.*

הָרַחֲמָן הוּא יְבָרֵךְ
אֶת אָבִי מוֹרִי בַּעַל
הַבַּיִת הַזֶּה, וְאֶת
אִמִּי מוֹרָתִי בַּעֲלַת
הַבַּיִת הַזֶּה, אוֹתָם
וְאֶת בֵּיתָם וְאֶת
זַרְעָם וְאֶת כָּל אֲשֶׁר
לָהֶם.

May the Merciful One bless my
father and my mother, heads of
this household, their children,
and all their family.

When eating at a communal meal:

Harahaman hu y'vareikh et kol ham'subin kan otanu v'et kol asher lanu.

הָרַחֲמָן הוּא יְבָרֵךְ אֶת כָּל הַמְסֻבִּין כָּאן אוֹתָנוּ וְאֶת כָּל אֲשֶׁר לָנוּ.

May the Merciful One bless all who are gathered here, us, and all that is ours.

Continue here:

כְּמוֹ שֶׁנִּתְבָּרְכוּ אֲבוֹתֵינוּ אַבְרָהָם יִצְחָק וְיַעֲקֹב, וּכְמוֹ שֶׁנִּתְבָּרְכוּ אִמּוֹתֵינוּ שָׂרָה רִבְקָה רָחֵל וְלֵאָה, בַּכֹּל מִכֹּל כֹּל. כֵּן יְבָרֵךְ אוֹתָנוּ כֻּלָּנוּ יַחַד בִּבְרָכָה שְׁלֵמָה וְנֹאמַר אָמֵן.

K'mo shenitbarkhu avoteinu Avraham, Yitzhak, v'Ya'akov, uk'mo shenitbarkhu imoteinu Sarah, Rivka, Rahel, v'Le-ah, bakol mikol kol. Kein y'vareikh otanu kulanu yahad bivrakhah sh'leimah v'nomar amein.

Just as our ancestors, Abraham, Isaac, Jacob, Sarah, Rebekah, Rachel, and Leah were blessed in every way, so may God bless all of us together with a perfect blessing, and let us say, Amen.

בַּמָּרוֹם יְלַמְּדוּ עֲלֵיהֶם
וְעָלֵינוּ זְכוּת שֶׁתְּהֵא
לְמִשְׁמֶרֶת שָׁלוֹם, וְנִשָּׂא
בְרָכָה מֵאֵת יְיָ, וּצְדָקָה
מֵאֱלֹהֵי יִשְׁעֵנוּ. וְנִמְצָא חֵן
וְשֵׂכֶל טוֹב בְּעֵינֵי אֱלֹהִים
וְאָדָם.

*Bamarom y'lamdu aleihem v'aleinu z'khut shet'hei
l'mishmeret shalom, v'nisah v'rakhah mei'eit Adonai
utz'dakah mei'Elohei yish'einu. V'nimtzah hein v'seikhel tov
b'einei Elohim v'adam.*

May our merit and the merit of our ancestors secure enduring
peace for all of us. May we receive a blessing from *Adonai* and
justice from the God who saves us. May we find grace and favor
from God and people.

Shabbat:

הָרַחֲמָן הוּא
יַנְחִילֵנוּ יוֹם שֶׁכֻּלוֹ
שַׁבָּת וּמְנוּחָה לְחַיֵּי
הָעוֹלָמִים.

*Harahaman hu yanhileinu
yom shekulo Shabbat
um'nuha l'hayei
ha'olamim.*

May the Merciful One give us a
day that is completely *Shabbat*,
and eternal rest in the world
to come.

Rosh Hodesh:

*Harahaman hu y'hadeish
aleinu et hahodesh hazeh
l'tovah v'livrakhah.*

May the Merciful One give
us this new month for
goodness and blessing.

הָרַחֲמָן הוּא
יְחַדֵּשׁ עָלֵינוּ אֶת
הַחֹדֶשׁ הַזֶּה לְטוֹבָה
וְלִבְרָכָה.

Pesah, Shavuot, and Sukkot:

*Harahaman hu yanhileinu
yom shekulo tov.*

May the Merciful One give us
a day that will be entirely good.

הָרַחֲמָן הוּא יַנְחִילֵנוּ
יוֹם שֶׁכֻּלּוֹ טוֹב.

Sukkot add:

*Harahaman hu yakim lanu
et sukkat David hanofalet.*

May the Merciful One erect the
fallen booth (Temple) of David
for us.

הָרַחֲמָן הוּא יָקִים
לָנוּ אֶת סֻכַּת דָּוִד
הַנּוֹפֶלֶת.

Rosh Hashanah:

*Harahaman hu y'hadesh
aleinu et hashanah hazot
l'tovah v'livrakhah.*

May the Merciful One give
us this year for goodness
and blessing.

הָרַחֲמָן הוּא
יְחַדֵּשׁ עָלֵינוּ אֶת
הַשָּׁנָה הַזֹּאת
לְטוֹבָה וְלִבְרָכָה.

For the State of Israel:

*Harahaman hu y'vareikh et
M'dinat Yisra'el, reishit
tz'mihat g'ulateinu.*

May the Merciful One bless the
State of Israel, the dawn of our
redemption.

הָרַחֲמָן הוּא יְבָרֵךְ
אֶת מְדִינַת יִשְׂרָאֵל
רֵאשִׁית צְמִיחַת
גְּאֻלָּתֵנוּ.

For Jews in crisis around the world:

*Harahaman hu y'vareikh et aheinu
b'nei Yisra'el han'tunim b'tzarah,
v'yotzi'eim mei'afeilah l'orah.*

May the Merciful One bless our
people who are in trouble and bring
them out of darkness into light.

הָרַחֲמָן הוּא יְבָרֵךְ
אֶת אַחֵינוּ
בְּנֵי יִשְׂרָאֵל הַנְּתוּנִים
בְּצָרָה, וְיוֹצִיאֵם
מֵאֲפֵלָה לְאוֹרָה.

For the Messiah:

*Harahaman hu y'zakeinu limot
haMashiah ulhayei ha'olam habah.*

May the Merciful One enable us
to live in the days of the Messiah
and in the world to come.

הָרַחֲמָן הוּא יְזַכֵּנוּ
לִימוֹת הַמָּשִׁיחַ
וּלְחַיֵּי הָעוֹלָם הַבָּא.

מִגְדוֹל יְשׁוּעוֹת מַלְכּוֹ וְעֹשֶׂה חֶסֶד לִמְשִׁיחוֹ,
לְדָוִד וּלְזַרְעוֹ עַד עוֹלָם. עוֹשֶׂה שָׁלוֹם בִּמְרוֹמָיו
הוּא יַעֲשֶׂה שָׁלוֹם עָלֵינוּ וְעַל כָּל יִשְׂרָאֵל,
וְאִמְרוּ אָמֵן.

*Migdol y'shu'ot malko v'oseh ḥesed limshiḥo, l'David ul'zaro
ad olam. Oseh shalom bimromav hu ya'aseh shalom aleinu
v'al kol Yisra'el, v'imru amein.*

God is a tower of strength to God's chosen ruler, and shows
kindness for God's anointed one, for David and his descendents
forever. May God who creates peace, create peace for us, for all
Israel, for everyone of earth, and let us say, Amen.

יְראוּ אֶת יְיָ קְדוֹשָׁיו כִּי אֵין מַחְסוֹר לִירֵאָיו.
כְּפִירִים רָשׁוּ וְרָעֵבוּ וְדוֹרְשֵׁי יְיָ לֹא יַחְסְרוּ
כָל טוֹב. הוֹדוּ לַיְיָ כִּי טוֹב, כִּי לְעוֹלָם חַסְדּוֹ.
פּוֹתֵחַ אֶת יָדֶךָ, וּמַשְׂבִּיעַ לְכָל חַי רָצוֹן.
בָּרוּךְ הַגֶּבֶר אֲשֶׁר יִבְטַח בַּיְיָ, וְהָיָה יְיָ מִבְטַחוֹ.
נַעַר הָיִיתִי גַּם זָקַנְתִּי, וְלֹא רָאִיתִי צַדִּיק נֶעֱזָב
וְזַרְעוֹ מְבַקֶּשׁ לָחֶם. יְיָ עֹז לְעַמּוֹ יִתֵּן יְיָ יְבָרֵךְ
אֶת עַמּוֹ בַשָּׁלוֹם.

*Yir'u et Adonai k'doshav ki ein mahsor lirei'av. K'firim rashu
v'ra'eivu v'dorshei Adonai lo yahs'ru khol tov. Hodu l'Adonai
ki tov, ki l'olam hasdo. Poteiah et yadekhah, umasbia l'khol
hai ratzon. Barukh hagever asher yivtah baAdonai, v'hayah
Adonai mivtaho. Na'ar hayiti gam zakanti, v'lo raiti tzadik
ne'ezav v'zar'o m'vakesh lahem. Adonai oz l'amo yitein
Adonai y'vareikh et amo vashalom.*

Respect *Adonai*, God's holy ones, for those who show respect to
God do not need anything. Scoffers may complain and go hungry,
but those who seek *Adonai* lack nothing good. Thank *Adonai*, for
God is good; for God's kindness endures forever. You open Your
hand and satisfy the desires of every living thing with favor.
Blessed is the person who trusts in *Adonai*, for God will be the
individual's protection. I have been young and now I am older, but I
have not seen a righteous person forgotten, nor a righteous
person's children begging for bread. *Adonai* will give strength to
God's people. *Adonai* will bless God's people with peace.

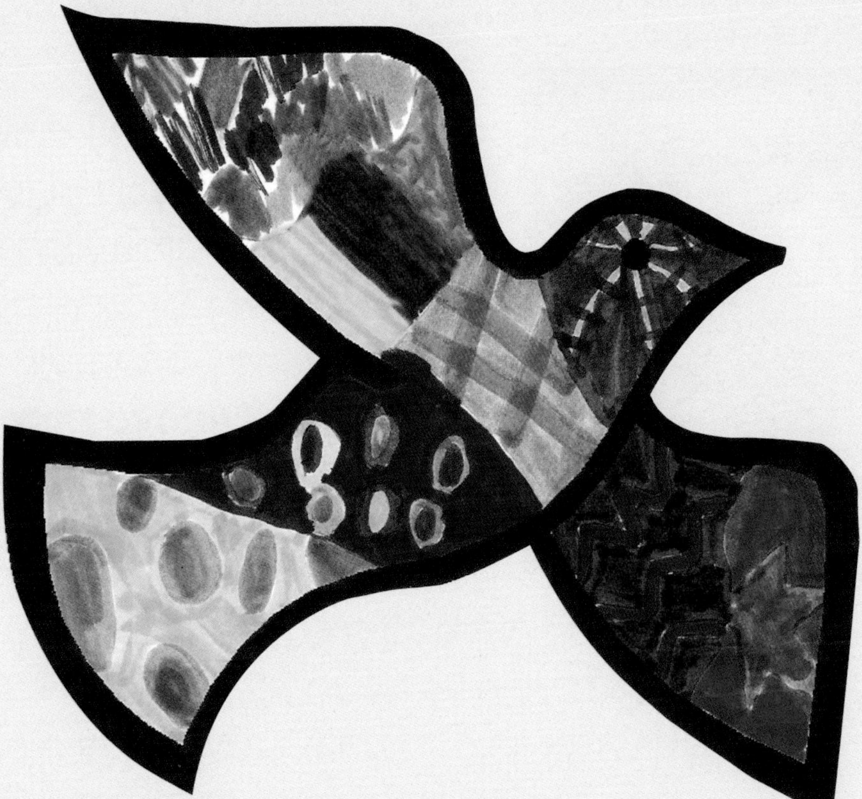

קִדּוּשׁ לְיוֹם שַׁבָּת

The *Kiddush* recited at *Shabbat* lunch emphasizes the everlasting covenant between God and the Jewish people. Just as God created the world and then rested, we too observe and enjoy this gift of *Shabbat* relaxation.

וְשָׁמְרוּ בְנֵי יִשְׂרָאֵל אֶת
הַשַּׁבָּת, לַעֲשׂוֹת אֶת הַשַּׁבָּת
לְדֹרֹתָם, בְּרִית עוֹלָם. בֵּינִי וּבֵין
בְּנֵי יִשְׂרָאֵל אוֹת הִיא לְעוֹלָם,
כִּי שֵׁשֶׁת יָמִים עָשָׂה יְיָ אֶת
הַשָּׁמַיִם וְאֶת הָאָרֶץ,
וּבַיּוֹם הַשְּׁבִיעִי שָׁבַת וַיִּנָּפַשׁ.

זָכוֹר אֶת יוֹם הַשַּׁבָּת לְקַדְּשׁוֹ.
שֵׁשֶׁת יָמִים תַּעֲבֹד וְעָשִׂיתָ כָּל מְלַאכְתֶּךָ. וְיוֹם הַשְּׁבִיעִי
שַׁבָּת לַיְיָ אֱלֹהֶיךָ, לֹא תַעֲשֶׂה כָל מְלָאכָה, אַתָּה וּבִנְךָ
וּבִתֶּךָ, עַבְדְּךָ וַאֲמָתְךָ וּבְהֶמְתֶּךָ, וְגֵרְךָ אֲשֶׁר בִּשְׁעָרֶיךָ.
כִּי שֵׁשֶׁת יָמִים עָשָׂה יְיָ אֶת הַשָּׁמַיִם וְאֶת הָאָרֶץ,
אֶת הַיָּם וְאֶת כָּל אֲשֶׁר בָּם, וַיָּנַח בַּיּוֹם הַשְּׁבִיעִי.

עַל כֵּן בֵּרַךְ יְיָ אֶת יוֹם הַשַּׁבָּת וַיְקַדְּשֵׁהוּ.

Exodus 31:16-17 and 20:8-11

סַבְרִי חֲבֵרַי:
בָּרוּךְ אַתָּה יְיָ אֱלֹהֵינוּ מֶלֶךְ הָעוֹלָם, בּוֹרֵא פְּרִי הַגָּפֶן.

V'shamru v'nei Yisra'el et haShabbat, la'asot et haShabbat l'dorotam, b'rit olam. Beini uvein b'nei Yisra'el ot hi l'olam, ki sheishet yamim asah Adonai et hashamayim v'et ha'aretz, uvayom hash'vi'i shavat va-yinafash.

Zakhor et yom haShabbat l'kadsho. Sheishet yamim ta'avod v'asitah kol m'lakhtekhah. V'yom hash'vi-i Shabbat l'Adonai Elohekhah, lo ta'aseh khol m'lakhah, atah uvinkha uvitekhah, avd'khah va'amatkhah uvhemt'khah, v'gerkhah asher bish'arekhah. Ki sheishet yamim asah Adonai et hashamayim v'et ha'aretz, et hayam v'et kol asher bam, vayana<u>h</u> bayom hashvi'i. Al kein beirakh Adonai et yom haShabbat vay'kad'sheihu.

Savri <u>h</u>aveirai:
Barukh atah Adonai Eloheinu melekh ha'olam, borei p'ri hagafen.

The people of Israel shall celebrate *Shabbat* throughout their generations as an everlasting covenant. It is a sign between Me and the people of Israel forever that in six days *Adonai* made heaven and earth, and on the seventh day God ceased from God's work and rested.

Remember to make *Shabbat* holy. Six days you shall do all your work. But the seventh day is a *Shabbat* to *Adonai* your God, on it you shall not do any work—you, your son or your daughter, your workers, your animals, or the stranger who is among you. For in six days *Adonai* made heaven and earth, the sea and everything in it, and God rested on the seventh day. Therefore God blessed the seventh day and made it holy. Praised are You, *Adonai*, Ruler of the universe, Creator of the fruit of the vine.

Shabbat lunch continues with *N'tilat Yadayim, Hamotzi,* and singing *Z'mirot.* After we conclude *Shabbat* lunch, we thank *Adonai* and those who prepared our meal with *Birkat HaMazon* that begins with *Shir Hama'lot* on page 44.

• Discuss *Parshat Hashavua,* this week's *Torah* portion over lunch.

Havdalah

הַבְדָּלָה

Concluding *Shabbat* and Holidays

When we see three stars in the night sky, we know *Shabbat* has come to an end. Although we are saddened that *Shabbat* must depart, we honor it with a special farewell ceremony, *Havdalah* (separation). We fill and drink a cup of wine or grape juice. We received a *neshamah yetayrah* (extra soul) as *Shabbat* began and now it departs to return next week. Sweet smelling spices help cushion our sadness. The *Havdalah* candle, made of at least two braided wicks, is lit and held high. We dim the lights, drawing attention to the evening's darkness all around us as we welcome the beginning of a new day and work week.

· What are you looking forward to in the coming week?

· What will you do this week to make our world more peaceful?

הִנֵּה אֵל יְשׁוּעָתִי,
אֶבְטַח וְלֹא אֶפְחָד.
כִּי עָזִּי וְזִמְרָת יָהּ יְיָ,
וַיְהִי לִי לִישׁוּעָה.
וּשְׁאַבְתֶּם מַיִם בְּשָׂשׂוֹן
מִמַּעַיְנֵי הַיְשׁוּעָה. לַיְיָ הַיְשׁוּעָה, עַל עַמְּךָ
בִרְכָתֶךָ, סֶּלָה. יְיָ צְבָאוֹת עִמָּנוּ, מִשְׂגָּב לָנוּ
אֱלֹהֵי יַעֲקֹב, סֶלָה. יְיָ צְבָאוֹת, אַשְׁרֵי אָדָם
בֹּטֵחַ בָּךְ. יְיָ הוֹשִׁיעָה, הַמֶּלֶךְ יַעֲנֵנוּ בְיוֹם קָרְאֵנוּ.

All:

לַיְהוּדִים הָיְתָה אוֹרָה וְשִׂמְחָה
וְשָׂשׂוֹן וִיקָר. כֵּן תִּהְיֶה לָנוּ.

Leader lifts the cup and says:

כּוֹס יְשׁוּעוֹת אֶשָּׂא וּבְשֵׁם יְיָ אֶקְרָא.

Hinei Eil y'shu'ati evtah v'lo efhad. Ki ozi v'zimrat Yah Adonai, va-y'hi li lishu'ah. Ush'avtem mayim b'sason mima'ayanei hay'shu'ah. L'Adonai hay'shu'ah, al amkhah birkhatekhah, selah. Adonai tz'va'ot imanu, misgav lanu Elohei Ya'akov, selah. Adonai tz'va'ot, ashrei adam boteah bakh. Adonai hoshi'ah, hamelekh ya'aneinu v'yom kor'einu.

All: *Lay'hudim ha-y'tah orah v'simha v'sason vikar. Kein tih'yeh lanu.*

Leader lifts the cup and says: *Kos y'shu'ot esah uv'sheim Adonai ekrah.*

Behold, my God of help, in whom I trust, and I am not afraid. *Adonai* is my strength and song; God is my Deliverer. With joy will you draw water out of the wells of salvation. *Adonai* alone is our help; God will bless God's people. *Adonai* of the universe is with us; the God of Jacob is our protection. *Adonai* of the universe, happy is the person who trusts in You. God who saves, the Ruler who will answer us on the day we call.

All: There was light and joy, gladness and honor for the Jewish people. So may we be blessed.

Leader lifts the cup and says: I will lift the cup of salvation and call upon the name of *Adonai*.

Wait to drink from it until the end of *Havdalah* blessing:

סָבְרִי חֲבֵרַי:

בָּרוּךְ אַתָּה יְיָ אֱלֹהֵינוּ מֶלֶךְ הָעוֹלָם,
בּוֹרֵא פְּרִי הַגָּפֶן.

Barukh atah Adonai Eloheinu melekh ha'olam, borei p'ri hagafen.

Praised are You, *Adonai* our God, Ruler of the universe, Creator of the fruit of the vine.

Lift the spices, recite the *brakhah* and then breathe in the fragrance:

בָּרוּךְ אַתָּה יְיָ אֱלֹהֵינוּ מֶלֶךְ הָעוֹלָם,
בּוֹרֵא מִינֵי בְשָׂמִים.

Barukh atah Adonai Eloheinu melekh ha'olam, borei minei v'samim.

Praised are You, *Adonai* our God, Ruler of the universe, Creator of various spices.

Examine your fingers in the light of the flame and recite:

בָּרוּךְ אַתָּה יְיָ אֱלֹהֵינוּ מֶלֶךְ הָעוֹלָם,
בּוֹרֵא מְאוֹרֵי הָאֵשׁ.

Barukh atah Adonai Eloheinu melekh ha'olam, borei m'orei ha'eish.

Praised are You, *Adonai* our God, Ruler of the universe, Creator of the lights of fire.

בָּרוּךְ אַתָּה יְיָ אֱלֹהֵינוּ מֶלֶךְ הָעוֹלָם, הַמַּבְדִּיל בֵּין קֹדֶשׁ לְחוֹל, בֵּין אוֹר לְחֹשֶׁךְ, בֵּין יִשְׂרָאֵל לָעַמִּים, בֵּין יוֹם הַשְּׁבִיעִי לְשֵׁשֶׁת יְמֵי הַמַּעֲשֶׂה. בָּרוּךְ אַתָּה יְיָ, הַמַּבְדִּיל בֵּין קֹדֶשׁ לְחוֹל.

Drink, then pour out a little wine on a plate and extinguish the flame.

Barukh atah Adonai Eloheinu melekh ha'olam, hamavdil bein kodesh l'hol, bein or l'hoshekh, bein Yisra'el la'amim, bein yom hash'vi'i l'sheishet y'mei hama'aseh. Barukh atah Adonai, hamavdil bein kodesh l'hol.

Praised are You, *Adonai* our God, Ruler of the universe, who has made a distinction between holy and regular time, between light and darkness, between the people of Israel and other nations, between the seventh day and the six days of the work week. Praised are You, *Adonai*, who distinguishes between holy and regular time.

הַמַּבְדִּיל בֵּין קֹדֶשׁ לְחוֹל, חַטֹּאתֵינוּ הוּא יִמְחֹל, זַרְעֵנוּ וְכַסְפֵּנוּ יַרְבֶּה כַחוֹל וְכַכּוֹכָבִים בַּלַּיְלָה. שָׁבוּעַ טוֹב.

Hamavdil bein kodesh l'hol, hatoteinu hu yimhol, zareinu v'khas'peinu yar'beh khahol v'khakokhavim ba'lay'lah. Shavuah tov!

God separates sacred and regular time; may God forgive our sins, may God increase our families and resources like grains of sand, like stars up in the sky. Have a good week!

To mark the conclusion of holidays, recite only the blessing over the wine and the concluding paragraph of *Havdalah.*

We conclude *Havdalah* by welcoming Elijah the prophet and Miriam the prophetess who will announce the coming of better days.

אֵלִיָּהוּ הַנָּבִיא, אֵלִיָּהוּ הַתִּשְׁבִּי,
אֵלִיָּהוּ, אֵלִיָּהוּ, אֵלִיָּהוּ, הַגִּלְעָדִי.
בִּמְהֵרָה בְיָמֵינוּ יָבֹא אֵלֵינוּ
עִם מָשִׁיחַ בֶּן דָּוִד, עִם מָשִׁיחַ בֶּן דָּוִד.

Eliyahu hanavi, Eliyahu hatishbi, Eliyahu, Eliyahu, Eliyahu hagil'adi. Bimheirah v'yameinu, yavo eileinu im Mashiah ben David, im Mashiah ben David.

May the prophet Elijah come soon, in our time, with the Messiah, son of David.

מִרְיָם הַנְּבִיאָה
עֹז וְזִמְרָה בְּיָדָהּ
מִרְיָם תִּרְקֹד אִתָּנוּ
לְהַגְדִּיל זִמְרַת עוֹלָם.
מִרְיָם תִּרְקֹד אִתָּנוּ
לְתַקֵּן אֶת הָעוֹלָם.
בִּמְהֵרָה בְיָמֵינוּ
הִיא תְּבִיאֵנוּ אֶל מֵי הַיְשׁוּעָה.

Miryam han'vi'ah oz v'zimrah b'yadah. Miryam tirkod itanu l'hagdil zimrat olam. Miryam tirkod itanu l'takein et ha'olam. Bimheirah v'yameinu hi t'vi'einu el mei ha-y'shu'ah.

Miriam the prophet, with her timbrel in her hand. Miriam will dance with us to strengthen the world's song. Miriam will dance with us to help repair the world. She will bring us to the waters of redemption.

הַדְלָקַת נֵרוֹת לְיוֹם טוֹב   *Hadlakat Neirot L'Yom Tov*

Lighting Festival Candles

On *Pesah*, *Shavuot*, *Sukkot*, and *Rosh Hashanah* we recite this blessing as we light the festival candles. When the festival occurs on *Shabbat*, we add the words in brackets and cover our eyes. On *Shabbat* lighting a fire is traditionally forbidden, while on a festival one can transfer a flame to cook. This is also the reason a candle is not used during *Havdalah* at the conclusion of a festival. On these Festivals and on *Yom Kippur* we also recite the *Sheheheyanu brakhah* on page 81.

בָּרוּךְ אַתָּה יְיָ אֱלֹהֵינוּ מֶלֶךְ הָעוֹלָם,
אֲשֶׁר קִדְּשָׁנוּ בְּמִצְוֹתָיו וְצִוָּנוּ,
לְהַדְלִיק נֵר שֶׁל (שַׁבָּת וְ) יוֹם טוֹב.

Barukh atah Adonai Eloheinu melekh ha'olam, asher kid'shanu b'mitzvotav v'tzivanu, l'hadlik neir shel (Shabbat v') Yom Tov.

Praised are You, *Adonai*, our God, Ruler of the universe, who makes us holy through Your *mitzvot*, and commands us to light the (*Shabbat* and) Festival candles.

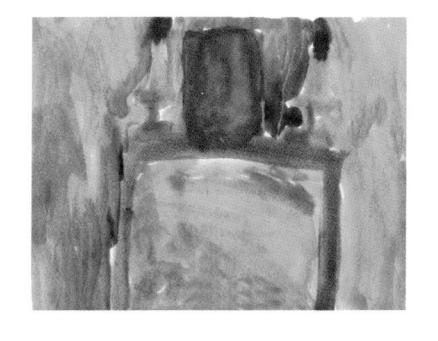

Yom Kippur:

בָּרוּךְ אַתָּה יְיָ אֱלֹהֵינוּ מֶלֶךְ הָעוֹלָם,
אֲשֶׁר קִדְּשָׁנוּ בְּמִצְוֹתָיו וְצִוָּנוּ,
לְהַדְלִיק נֵר שֶׁל (שַׁבָּת וְ) יוֹם הַכִּפּוּרִים.

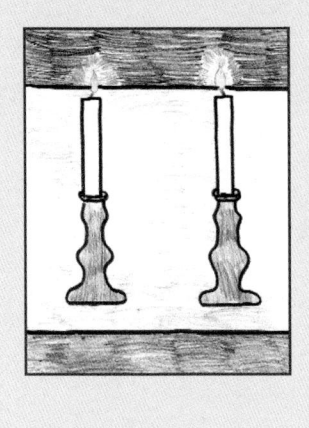

*Barukh atah Adonai Eloheinu melekh
ha'olam, asher kid'shanu b'mitzvotav
v'tzivanu, l'hadlik neir shel (Shabbat v')
Yom HaKipurim.*

Praised are You, *Adonai*, our God, Ruler of
the universe, who makes us holy through
Your *mitzvot*, and commands us to light the
(*Shabbat* and) *Yom Kippur* candles.

שֶׁהֶחֱיָנוּ

Sheheḥeyanu

On all festivals except the last two nights of *Pesaḥ* we recite the
Sheheḥeyanu brakhah thanking God for giving us this new
opportunity to rejoice on this holiday.

בָּרוּךְ אַתָּה יְיָ אֱלֹהֵינוּ מֶלֶךְ הָעוֹלָם,
שֶׁהֶחֱיָנוּ וְקִיְּמָנוּ וְהִגִּיעָנוּ לַזְּמַן הַזֶּה.

*Barukh atah Adonai Eloheinu melekh ha'olam, sheheḥeyanu
v'kiy'manu v'higi'anu laz'man hazeh.*

Praised are You, *Adonai*, our God, Ruler of the universe, who gives
us life, sustains us, and enables us to reach this day.

· What words of blessing do you want to offer your family, friends,
  and God on this special day?

Kiddush L'Leil Yom Tov

קִדּוּשׁ לְלֵיל יוֹם טוֹב

Kiddush for Festival Evening

The Festival evening *Kiddush* celebrates God's connection to the Jewish people through our important historical events and holidays. We are God's partners in bringing holiness into the world. For Festival evenings that occur on *Shabbat*, add the words in the parenthesis and this Biblical passage celebrating creation.

Shabbat:

וַיְהִי עֶרֶב וַיְהִי בְקֶר יוֹם הַשִּׁשִּׁי.

וַיְכֻלּוּ הַשָּׁמַיִם וְהָאָרֶץ וְכָל צְבָאָם.

וַיְכַל אֱלֹהִים בַּיּוֹם הַשְּׁבִיעִי

מְלַאכְתּוֹ אֲשֶׁר עָשָׂה,

וַיִּשְׁבֹּת בַּיּוֹם הַשְּׁבִיעִי מִכָּל

מְלַאכְתּוֹ אֲשֶׁר עָשָׂה.

וַיְבָרֶךְ אֱלֹהִים

אֶת יוֹם הַשְּׁבִיעִי

וַיְקַדֵּשׁ אֹתוֹ,

כִּי בוֹ שָׁבַת מִכָּל מְלַאכְתּוֹ

אֲשֶׁר בָּרָא אֱלֹהִים לַעֲשׂוֹת.

Genesis 1:31-2:3

Shabbat and Festivals:

סַבְרִי חֲבֵרִי:

בָּרוּךְ אַתָּה יְיָ אֱלֹהֵינוּ מֶלֶךְ הָעוֹלָם,

בּוֹרֵא פְּרִי הַגָּפֶן.

בָּרוּךְ אַתָּה יְיָ אֱלֹהֵינוּ מֶלֶךְ הָעוֹלָם, אֲשֶׁר בָּחַר בָּנוּ מִכָּל עָם וְרוֹמְמָנוּ מִכָּל לָשׁוֹן, וְקִדְּשָׁנוּ בְּמִצְוֹתָיו. וַתִּתֶּן לָנוּ יְיָ אֱלֹהֵינוּ בְּאַהֲבָה (שַׁבָּתוֹת לִמְנוּחָה וּ) מוֹעֲדִים לְשִׂמְחָה, חַגִּים וּזְמַנִּים לְשָׂשׂוֹן, אֶת יוֹם (הַשַּׁבָּת הַזֶּה וְאֶת יוֹם)

Sukkot:	Shavuot:	Pesaḥ:
חַג הַסֻּכּוֹת	חַג הַשָּׁבוּעוֹת	חַג הַמַּצּוֹת
הַזֶּה, זְמַן	הַזֶּה, זְמַן מַתַּן	הַזֶּה, זְמַן
שִׂמְחָתֵנוּ,	תּוֹרָתֵנוּ,	חֵרוּתֵנוּ,

Sh'mini Atzeret and Simḥat Torah:

הַשְּׁמִינִי, חַג הָעֲצֶרֶת הַזֶּה, זְמַן שִׂמְחָתֵנוּ,

(בְּאַהֲבָה) מִקְרָא קֹדֶשׁ, זֵכֶר לִיצִיאַת מִצְרָיִם. כִּי בָנוּ בָחַרְתָּ וְאוֹתָנוּ קִדַּשְׁתָּ מִכָּל הָעַמִּים, וְשַׁבָּת) וּמוֹעֲדֵי קָדְשֶׁךָ (בְּאַהֲבָה וּבְרָצוֹן) בְּשִׂמְחָה וּבְשָׂשׂוֹן הִנְחַלְתָּנוּ. בָּרוּךְ אַתָּה יְיָ, מְקַדֵּשׁ (הַשַּׁבָּת וְ) יִשְׂרָאֵל וְהַזְּמַנִּים.

On Saturday night to separate *Shabbat* from the Festival, continue
with this shortened *Havdalah* service. Hold the candle high in the
air, examine your fingers in the light of the flame, and recite:

בָּרוּךְ אַתָּה יְיָ אֱלֹהֵינוּ מֶלֶךְ הָעוֹלָם,
בּוֹרֵא מְאוֹרֵי הָאֵשׁ.

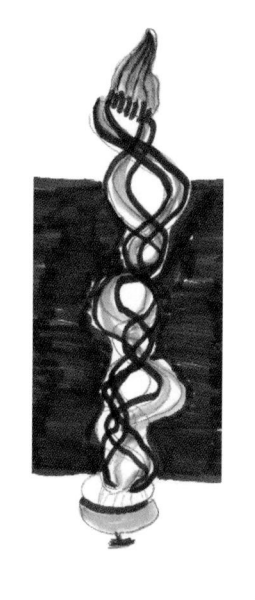

בָּרוּךְ אַתָּה יְיָ אֱלֹהֵינוּ מֶלֶךְ הָעוֹלָם,
הַמַּבְדִּיל בֵּין קֹדֶשׁ לְחוֹל,
בֵּין אוֹר לְחֹשֶׁךְ,
בֵּין יִשְׂרָאֵל לָעַמִּים,
בֵּין יוֹם הַשְּׁבִיעִי
לְשֵׁשֶׁת יְמֵי הַמַּעֲשֶׂה.
בֵּין קְדֻשַּׁת שַׁבָּת לִקְדֻשַּׁת
יוֹם טוֹב הִבְדַּלְתָּ,
וְאֶת יוֹם הַשְּׁבִיעִי מִשֵּׁשֶׁת
יְמֵי הַמַּעֲשֶׂה קִדַּשְׁתָּ,
הִבְדַּלְתָּ וְקִדַּשְׁתָּ אֶת עַמְּךָ יִשְׂרָאֵל בִּקְדֻשָּׁתֶךָ.
בָּרוּךְ אַתָּה יְיָ הַמַּבְדִּיל בֵּין קֹדֶשׁ לְקֹדֶשׁ.

On *Sukkot* we recite this blessing every time we eat in a *sukkah*.
On the first night of *Sukkot*, recite this *brakhah* in the *sukkah* and
then *Sheheheyanu*.

בָּרוּךְ אַתָּה יְיָ אֱלֹהֵינוּ מֶלֶךְ הָעוֹלָם,
אֲשֶׁר קִדְּשָׁנוּ בְּמִצְוֹתָיו, וְצִוָּנוּ לֵישֵׁב בַּסֻּכָּה.

*Barukh atah Adonai Eloheinu melekh ha'olam, asher kid'shanu
b'mitzvotav v'tzivanu leisheiv basukkah.*

Praised are You, *Adonai*, our God, Ruler of the universe, who makes
us holy through Your *mitzvot*, and commands us to sit in a *sukkah*.

On the second night of *Sukkot*, recite *Sheheheyanu*
and then the *brakhah* for sitting in the *sukkah*:

Sheheheyanu is recited on holidays except on the seventh day of *Pesah*:

בָּרוּךְ אַתָּה יְיָ אֱלֹהֵינוּ מֶלֶךְ הָעוֹלָם,
שֶׁהֶחֱיָנוּ וְקִיְּמָנוּ וְהִגִּיעָנוּ לַזְּמַן הַזֶּה.

Shabbat:

*Vay'hi erev vay'hi voker yom hashishi. Vay'khulu hashamayim
veha'aretz vekhol tz'va'am. Vay'khal Elohim bayom hash'vi'i
m'lakhto asher asah, vayishbot bayom hash'vi'i mikol m'lakhto
asher asah. Vay'vareikh Elohim et yom hashvi'i vay'kadesh oto, ki
vo shavat mikol m'lakhto asher barah Elohim la'asot.*

When the festival doesn't begin on *Shabbat, Kiddush* starts here:

Savri haveirai:

*Barukh atah Adonai Eloheinu melekh ha'olam, borei p'ri hagafen.
Barukh atah Adonai Eloheinu melekh ha'olam, asher bahar banu mikol
am v'rom'manu mikol lashon, v'kid'shanu b'mitz'votav. Vatiten lanu
Adonai Eloheinu b'ahavah (Shabbatot lim'nuhah u) mo'adim l'simhah,
hagim uz'manim l'sason, et yom (haShabbat hazeh v'et yom)*

Pesah	*Shavuot:*	*Sukkot:*
Hag Hamatzot hazeh, z'man heiruteinu,	*Hag Hashavu'ot hazeh, z'man matan Torateinu,*	*Hag Hasukkot hazeh, z'man simhateinu,*

Shemini Atzeret and Simhat Torah:
Hash'mini, Hag Ha'atzeret hazeh, z'man simhateinu,

*(b'ahavah) mikrah kodesh, zeikher litzi'at mitzrayim. Ki vanu
vahartah v'otanu kidashtah mikol ha'amim, (v'Shabbat) umo'adei
kodsh'khah (b'ahavah uv'ratzon) b'simhah uv'sason hinhaltanu.
Barukh atah Adonai, m'kadesh (haShabbat v') Yisra'el v'haz'manim.*

On Saturday night recite:
Barukh atah Adonai Eloheinu melekh ha'olam, borei m'orei ha'eish.

Barukh atah Adonai Eloheinu melekh ha'olam, hamavdil bein kodesh l'hol, bein or l'hoshekh, bein Yisra'el la'amim, bein yom hash'vi'i l'sheishet y'mei hama'aseh. Bein k'dushat Shabbat lik'dushat Yom Tov hivdaltah, v'et yom hash'vi'i misheishet y'mei ha'ma'aseh kidashtah, hivdaltah v'kidashtah et amkhah Yisra'el bik'dushatekhah. Barukh atah Adonai, hamavdil bein kodesh l'kodesh.

Continue with *Sheheheyanu* except on the seventh and eighth days of *Pesah*.

Barukh atah Adonai Eloheinu melekh ha'olam, sheheheyanu v'kiy'manu v'higi'anu laz'man hazeh.

Shabbat:

"And there was evening and there was morning: the sixth day. The heavens and the earth, and all their contents were completed. On the seventh day God completed all the skilled work. God ceased from all God's work. God blessed the seventh day and declared it holy because on that day God rested from all the acts of creation."   *Genesis 1:31-2:3*

Praised are You, *Adonai*, our God, Ruler of the universe, Creator of the fruit of the vine.

Festivals:

Praised are You, *Adonai*, our God, Ruler of the universe, who chose and distinguished us from among all others by adding holiness to our lives with Your *mitzvot*. Lovingly, You gave us the gift of (*Shabbat* for rest and) Festivals for joy and holidays for happiness, among them (this *Shabbat* and) this day of

Pesah	*Shavuot:*	*Sukkot:*
Pesah, the time of our liberation,	*Shavuot*, the time of Your giving us the *Torah*	*Sukkot*, the time of our joy,

Sh'mini Atzeret and *Simhat Torah*:
Sh'mini Atzeret, the time of our joy,

a day of holy gathering recalling the Exodus from Egypt. You choose us, endowing us with holiness from among all peoples, by giving us (*Shabbat* and) Your holy Festivals (lovingly and gladly) in happiness and joy. Praised are You, *Adonai*, who makes holy (*Shabbat* and) the people Israel and the Festivals.

Saturday night:

Praised are You, *Adonai* our God, Ruler of the universe, creator of the lights of the fire. Praised are You, *Adonai* our God, Ruler of the universe, who gave all creation distinctive qualities, distinguishing between holy and secular time, between light and darkness, between the people Israel and other peoples, between the seventh day and the six working days of the week. You made a distinction between the holiness of *Shabbat* and the holiness of Festivals, and You made *Shabbat* more holy than the other days of the week. You set Your people Israel apart, making their lives holy through Your holiness. Praised are You, *Adonai*, who distinguishes one holy time from another holy time.

Praised are You, *Adonai* our God, Ruler of the universe, for giving us life, sustaining us, and helping us reach this day.

We continue with *N'tilat Yadayim*, *Hamotzi*, and singing *Z'mirot* beginning on page 28. After we conclude our festival meal, we thank *Adonai* and those who prepared our meal with *Birkat HaMazon* on page 44.

קִדּוּשׁ לְיוֹם טוֹב

Kiddush L'Yom Tov

Kiddush for Festival Day

For Festival days that occur on *Shabbat* add the words in the parenthesis and this Biblical passage. We celebrate the creation of the world and the everlasting covenant between God and the Jewish people.

Shabbat:

וְשָׁמְרוּ בְנֵי יִשְׂרָאֵל אֶת הַשַּׁבָּת,
לַעֲשׂוֹת אֶת הַשַּׁבָּת לְדֹרֹתָם, בְּרִית עוֹלָם.
בֵּינִי וּבֵין בְּנֵי יִשְׂרָאֵל אוֹת הִיא לְעֹלָם,
כִּי שֵׁשֶׁת יָמִים עָשָׂה יְיָ אֶת הַשָּׁמַיִם
וְאֶת הָאָרֶץ, וּבַיּוֹם הַשְּׁבִיעִי שָׁבַת וַיִּנָּפַשׁ.

זָכוֹר אֶת יוֹם הַשַּׁבָּת לְקַדְּשׁוֹ. שֵׁשֶׁת יָמִים
תַּעֲבֹד וְעָשִׂיתָ כָּל מְלַאכְתֶּךָ. וְיוֹם הַשְּׁבִיעִי
שַׁבָּת לַיְיָ אֱלֹהֶיךָ, לֹא תַעֲשֶׂה כָל מְלָאכָה,
אַתָּה וּבִנְךָ וּבִתֶּךָ, עַבְדְּךָ וַאֲמָתְךָ וּבְהֶמְתֶּךָ,
וְגֵרְךָ אֲשֶׁר בִּשְׁעָרֶיךָ. כִּי שֵׁשֶׁת יָמִים עָשָׂה יְיָ
אֶת הַשָּׁמַיִם וְאֶת הָאָרֶץ, אֶת
הַיָּם וְאֶת כָּל אֲשֶׁר בָּם,
וַיָּנַח בַּיּוֹם הַשְּׁבִיעִי.

עַל כֵּן בֵּרַךְ יְיָ אֶת יוֹם
הַשַּׁבָּת וַיְקַדְּשֵׁהוּ.

Exodus 31:16-17 and Exodus 20:8-11

Festivals:

וַיְדַבֵּר מֹשֶׁה אֶת מוֹעֲדֵי יְיָ אֶל בְּנֵי יִשְׂרָאֵל.

Leviticus 23:44

סַבְרִי חֲבֵרִי:

בָּרוּךְ אַתָּה יְיָ אֱלֹהֵינוּ מֶלֶךְ הָעוֹלָם,

בּוֹרֵא פְּרִי הַגָּפֶן.

On *Sukkot* add the *brakhah* for sitting in the *sukkah* on page 84.

Shabbat:

*V'shamru v'nei Yisra'el et haShabbat, la'a'sot et haShabbat
l'dorotam, b'rit olam. Beini u'vein b'nei Yisra'el ot hi l'olam, ki
sheishet yamim asah Adonai et hashamayim v'et ha'aretz, u'vayom
hash'vi'i shavat va'yinafash.*

*Zakhor et yom haShabbat l'kad'sho. Sheishet yamim ta'avod v'asita
kol m'lakhtekhah. V'yom hashvi'i Shabbat l'Adonai Elohekhah, lo
ta'aseh khol m'lakhah, atah u'vinkhah uvitekhah, avd'khah
va'amatkhah u'vhemtekhah, v'gerkhah asher bish'arekhah. Ki
sheishet yamim asah Adonai et hashamayim v'et ha'aretz, et
hayam v'et kol asher bam, vayana̲h̲ bayom hash'vi'i. Al kein beirakh
Adonai et yom haShabbat vay'kad'sheihu.*

Festivals:

*Vay'daber Moshe et mo'adei Adonai el
b'nei Yisrael.*

Savri ha̲veirai:

*Barukh atah Adonai Eloheinu melekh
ha'olam, borei p'ri hagafen.*

Shabbat:

The people of Israel shall celebrate *Shabbat* throughout their generations as a everlasting covenant. It is a sign between Me and the people of Israel forever that in six days *Adonai* made heaven and earth, and on the seventh day God ceased from God's work and rested.

Remember to make *Shabbat* holy. Six days you shall do all your work. But the seventh day is a *Shabbat* to *Adonai* your God; on it you shall not do any work—you, your son or your daughter, your workers, your animals, or the stranger who is among you. For in six days *Adonai* made heaven and earth, the sea and everything in it, and God rested on the seventh day. Therefore God blessed *Shabbat* and made it holy.

Festivals:

Moses announced *Adonai's* festival times to the children of Israel.

Leviticus 23:44

Shabbat and Festivals:

Praised are You, *Adonai*, our God, Ruler of the universe, Creator of the fruit of the vine.

Our Festival lunch continues with *N'tilat Yadayim, Hamotzi*,and singing *Z'mirot* beginning on page 28. After we conclude our Festival lunch, we thank *Adonai* and those who prepared our meal with *Birkat HaMazon* on page 44.

קְרִיאַת שְׁמַע עַל הַמִּטָה

Kri'at Sh'ma Al Hamitah

Children's Bedtime Rituals

Reciting the *Shema* is a soothing, spiritual way to help your children prepare for sleep. Invite them to share the highs and lows of their day.

· What *Torah* insight did she learn today?

· Who are the people he wants to bless before going to sleep?

· Who are the people she wants to pray for their renewed health?

· What is he looking forward to in the morning?

 שְׁמַע יִשְׂרָאֵל, יְיָ אֱלֹהֵינוּ, יְיָ אֶחָד.

Recite softly:

בָּרוּךְ שֵׁם כְּבוֹד מַלְכוּתוֹ לְעוֹלָם וָעֶד.

וְאָהַבְתָּ אֵת יְיָ אֱלֹהֶיךָ
בְּכָל לְבָבְךָ וּבְכָל נַפְשְׁךָ וּבְכָל מְאֹדֶךָ.
וְהָיוּ הַדְּבָרִים הָאֵלֶּה
אֲשֶׁר אָנֹכִי מְצַוְּךָ הַיּוֹם עַל לְבָבֶךָ.
וְשִׁנַּנְתָּם לְבָנֶיךָ וְדִבַּרְתָּ בָּם
בְּשִׁבְתְּךָ בְּבֵיתֶךָ וּבְלֶכְתְּךָ בַדֶּרֶךְ
וּבְשָׁכְבְּךָ וּבְקוּמֶךָ.
וּקְשַׁרְתָּם לְאוֹת עַל יָדֶךָ
וְהָיוּ לְטֹטָפֹת בֵּין עֵינֶיךָ.
וּכְתַבְתָּם עַל מְזֻזוֹת בֵּיתֶךָ וּבִשְׁעָרֶיךָ.

Sh'ma Yisra'el, Adonai Eloheinu, Adonai Ehad.

Recite softly:

Barukh sheim k'vod malkhuto l'olam va'ed.

V'ahavtah eit Adonai Elohekhah, b'khol l'vavkhah uv'khol nafsh'khah uv'khol m'odekhah. V'hayu had'varim ha'eileh, asher anokhi m'tzav'khah hayom al l'vavekhah. V'shinantam l'vanekhah, v'dibartah bam, b'shivt'khah b'veitekhah uv'lekht'khah vaderekh, uv'shokhb'khah uv'kumekhah. U'kshartam l'ot al yadekhah, v'hayu l'totafot bein einekhah. Ukh'tavtam al m'zuzot beitekhah uvish'arekhah.

Listen Israel, *Adonai* is our God, *Adonai* is the only One.

Recite softly:

Praised is God's name whose glorious presence will last forever.

And you shall love *Adonai*, your God, with all your heart, with all your soul, and with all your might. Place these words that I command you on this day in your heart. Teach them to your children and talk about them when you sit in your home, when you walk on the way, when you lie down to sleep, and when you rise up. Tie them (*tefillin*) as a symbol on your hands and between your eyes. Write them (*mezuzah*) on the doorposts of your house and on your gates.

Thank you to the following artists who help bring the meaning of Shabbat and Festival celebrations alive in this Companion through their illustrations created while students at the Minneapolis Jewish Day School:

Danielle Appleman p. 5 & 23, Florrie Barron p. 55, Jessica Beugen p. 49, Julia Birnberg p. 13, Ethan Carrier p. 40, Ivan Carrier p. 18, Michael Cera p. 77, Kim Coffino p. 51, Olivia Cornfield p. 75, Layna Crandell p. 43, Artis Curiskis p. 16, Gabe Daitzchman p. 88, David Dotterweich p. 63, Shoshana Engelson p. 36 & 60, Miriam Feingold p. 79, Benji Fischman p. 17, Shoshana Fischman p. 87, Danielle Fogelson p. 35 & 65, Mari Fromstein p. 79, Anna Glassman-Kaufman p. 37, Molly Goldfarb p. 12, Aaron Goldsteen p. 27, Rebecca Goldsteen cover & p. 74, Elana Graf p. 29, David Greenfield p. 69, Caleb Hausman p. 66, Sasha Hausman p. 35, Mickela Heilicher p. 64, Imara Hixon p. 15, Talia Hoffman p. 82, Dalya Kahn p. 77, Danny Kahn p. 42, Luiza Kieffer p. 84, Abbe Kirshbaum p. 39, Rachel Kozberg p. 93, Noah Kupritz p. 57, Mollie Lazar p. 66, Stephanie Lehman p. 76, Nicky Leveris p. 53, Andrew Leibman p. 47 & 56, Eli Livon p. 89, Hallie Mogelson p. 8 & 24, Natalie Nelson p. 32, Allisa Newman p. 37, Paige Newman p. 9, Jessica Noaman p. 87, Noa Parker p. 20, Sydney Payton p. 71, Polina Pekurovsky, p. 72, Ari Pepper p. 67, Adam Rafowitz p. 73, Mia Rafowitz p. 62 & 96, Daniel Raskin p. 34, Ora Raymond p. 77, Jonathan Ribnick p. 48, Sonia Robiner p. 81, Allie Rosen p. 42, Noah Rothman p. 80, Nina Shragg p. 38, Lisa Soumekh p. 45, Sam Stillman p. 11, Sophie Stillman p. 26, Shelly Tennenbaum p. 28, Sam Vinitsky p. 91, Elana Vlodover p. 68, and Rachel Wolfe p. 31.

Thank you to the following individuals who helped to edit, proof, and provide valuable feedback about the text, design, and layout of this Companion:

Rabbi David Abramson, Sara Bernstein, Betsy Birnberg, Debra and Yoni Bundt, Rabbi Norman Cohen, Dyanne Cooperman, Rabbi Alexander Davis, Beth Dworsky, Sharon Fischman, Shelley Fogelson, Patricia Freeman, Amy Geller, Audrey Goldfarb, Christine Hausman, Andrea Johnson, Rabbi Robert Kahn, Chad Kampe, Dr. Ray Levi, Dr. Yaakov Levi, Christine Levin, Robin Neidorf, Cantor Neil Newman, Rabbi Stacy Offner, Debra Olson, Aimee Orkin, Leslie Paskoff, Abbe Payton, Stacy Pinck, Robert Portnoe, Susan Scofield, Amy Stern, David Stillman, Kim Teplinsky, Victoria Thor, Jannette Wachs, Dana Beth Weisman, and Dori Weinstein.

Thank you to the following people who contributed financially to make the design and production of this Companion possible:

Mark Appelbaum and Yaffa Cohen-Appelbaum, Brad Birnberg and Stacy Pinck, Carl and Tammy Birnberg, Leon and Louann Bongard, Ed and Molly Cavin, Stu Crandell and Gayle Sherman-Crandell, Jancis Curiskis and Sara Weiner, Leigh, Ellery and Yaya Deschamps, Gus and Alecia Dotterweich, Richard and Linda Dworsky, William and Beth Dworsky, Esther Fabes, Joseph and Sharon Fischman, Micah and Michal Garber, Joel and Kimberly Gedan, David and Darcy Gilbert Burke, Alan Goldfarb and Nancy Joseph-Goldfarb, Mace and Audrey Goldfarb, Stuart and Bobbie Goldfarb, David Goldsteen and Marcia Cohodes, Av and Bari Gordon, Ann Hunegs, Jeff and Orlee Kahn, Irv and Karen Katz, Robert Kaufman and Debra Glassman, Mitchell and Faye Kaye, Carolyn Krall, George and Linda Kubinski, Craig and Riva Kupritz, Steve and Bonnie Lazar, Howard and Lisa Lederer, Marty Lederman and Betty Smithberg, Sidney and Joannie Levinsohn, Ronen and Karen Malka, Marilyn Marker, Richard and Cathy Mogelson, Marvin and Bev Moore, James Moscowitz and Amy Taswell, Rita Nathanson, Arnold Orloff and Anne Drake, B. Aaron Parker, Jim and Abbe Payton, Ben and Lillian Pilcher, Norman and Dorothy Pink, David and Mary Raskin, Michael and Susan Resnick, Jerry and Louise Ribnick, Jules and Gay Rosenthal, Sheldon and Carol Segal, Stan and Joyce Segelbaum, Jerel and Judy Shapiro, Rick and Helen Siegel, Benhoor and Brenda Soumekh, Stuart and Cindy Tapper, Stuart and Janette Wachs, Todd Werner and Naomi King-Smith, David and Lisa Wolfe, David and Amy Zaroff, Michael and Elly Zweigbaum

Thank you to David Grossman, Karen Iverson, and the staff of Grossman Design for the graphic layout and design.

Hebrew text used with permission of Davka Corporation.